WHILE YOU WAIT:

A Sportsman's Guide to Nature

D0763432

WHILE YOU WAIT:

Illustrations By
Michael DiGiorgio

Distributed by Winchester Press
220 Old New Brunswick Road CN1332
Piscataway, New Jersey 08854

A Sportsman's Guide to Nature

By
Cliff Hauptman

Stone Wall Press, Inc.
1241 30th Street N.W.
Washington, D.C. 20007

Published March 1984

Library of Congress Card Number 83-051087
ISBN 0-913276-47-2

To my father
from upon whose shoulders
I first learned to love the outdoors.

Table of

Contents

Fall

Winter

This book is for both men and women. Because I am a male, however, I have used masculine pronouns throughout the book and I have referred to all sportsmen, whether male or female, the same. I have no wish to alienate the many female sportsmen who may read this book, especially my wife or my friends, but in the interest of readable prose, please accept my style of writing and know that, in my heart if not in my book, I am as non-sexist as the day is long. Even in Alaska. In the summer.

INTRODUCTION

In this book you will find nothing about deer or grouse or bass or trout. The hunter or fisherman already knows about those subjects. They are his quarry and plenty of books have already been devoted to them. This book is about plants and birds and insects and other subjects that are as much a part of the sportsman's outdoor experiences as the deer and trout. Here is the opportunity for the sportsman to find out about things he has always seen outdoors and wondered about, not knowing where to go for an answer—or, to begin noticing things that have always been there for him to see, had he but known where to look and what to look for. All this can be done "while you wait."

Most of your time spent hunting and fishing is actually spent waiting: waiting for the deer to show up; waiting for the birds to come in; waiting to twitch the lure; waiting for the fish to strike; waiting for the hatch to start; waiting for the wind to die down, or pick up. During those golden hours of waiting a sportsman can devote some of his valuable time to discovering and appreciating some of those wondrous, small side-shows of nature.

This book is designed to be read either afield or at home. Care has been taken to give the interested reader useful, concise, insightful, easy-to-find, and often fascinating information about a variety of natural subjects without taking a lot of time away from the primary activity in progress: hunting or fishing. If a particular creature or subject in this book piques your interest beyond the scope of this book, you can further your knowledge by finding other, more comprehensive books on those particular subjects. This book will have served its purpose of starting you on your way, and I will be very happy.

The subjects I have chosen to write about reflect my own interests in natural history. There is considerable confusion about many aspects of the natural world—those things that are most common yet most often overlooked, and some things that are not so easily encountered but are worth looking for. I have tried to shed some light on these areas of confusion for you. You will notice that a large percentage of the entries relates to insects. Insects are more abundant than all the birds, mammals, and reptiles combined; they represent a similarly large proportion of the life on this planet. Another reason is that they are easy to watch.

They are usually not shy like mammals and birds, and they are generally not in any great hurry to go somewhere else. A final reason cannot be explained to anyone who is not yet fascinated by insects. Once you get over an innate discomfort you may feel towards insects and begin to really learn about them, you will know the third reason.

My hope is that the information and guidance contained within this book will become an integral part of your outdoors experiences; that they will enrich your times afield and, thereby, your life. My hope is that by helping you become more familiar with nature, your love and respect for it will increase so that by becoming a better naturalist you will become a better sportsman. Better sportsmen influence a better quality of hunting and fishing, which is linked, in turn, to a healthier natural environment in general. It is a cycle as natural as nature itself.

Spring

Spring

Caddis Worms

All trout fishermen should be familiar with caddis worms and their adult stage, caddisflies. Along with mayflies and stoneflies, caddisflies comprise some of the most important aquatic insect hatches upon which trout feed. Knowing something of their life history may be of use to the angler, and the activities of the caddis worms may even be of some interest to the non-angler.

The immature stage of the caddisfly is the caddis worm. It looks somewhat like the little white grub one finds in the ground while working in the garden, but its sides are fringed with feathery gills, for the caddis worm lives under water. It also lives inside a case that it constructs around itself; so you are unlikely to see a naked caddis worm unless you pull one out of its house. The cases are usually in the form of a tube, open at both ends, and constructed of either plant material, sand grains, small stones, or a combination of materials depending on the species and the habitat. In streams with good caddis populations, caddis worms in their cases can be found in abundance, especially upon submerged logs and rocks.

Some species of caddis worms do not construct cases, but rather spin nets of silk that catch tiny creatures and particles of food from the current.

Caddis worms pass through a pupal stage in their development. They seal themselves up in their cases and pupate until they are ready to emerge as adult caddisflies. They are often fed upon by trout during the migration from their pupal cases to the water's surface. And it is the flies that imitate this stage that are the most effective for fishing the caddis hatches.

Once the insect has broken out of its pupal skin at the water's surface, it flies away. Unlike mayflies, caddisflies spend almost no time floating on the surface. That is why fishing the subsurface, pupal imitations is more productive than the adult imitations during a hatch. Later, however, when the adult females return to the water to lay eggs, an adult caddisfly imitation skittered across the surface may bring a strike.

Adult caddisflies look very much like moths, but their antennae are very long and threadlike. Adult caddisflies are often referred to as "sedges."

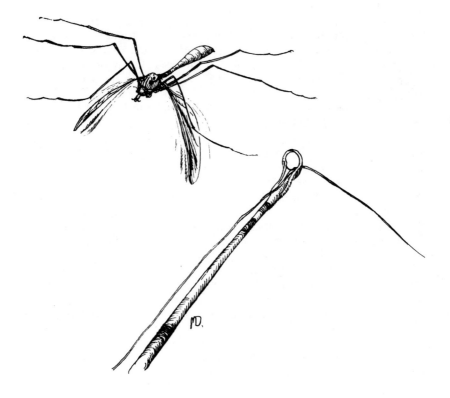

Crane Flies

Crane flies are those enormous mosquito-like creatures about two inches long, that look as though they could suck all the blood out of your body in one shot. Actually, though, they are not mosquitoes, they don't suck blood, and they are, despite their size, completely harmless.

These flies are related to mosquitoes, as are all true flies. True flies differ from all other kinds of insects in having only one pair of wings. All other winged, adult insects have two pairs of wings. The larvae of crane flies are wormlike creatures that live either under water or in moist environments underground. Many sportsmen know them as spikes or leatherjackets and use them as bait. Most crane fly larvae eat decaying plant material. Not much is known about what the adults eat. Most of the "skater" type dry flies are imitations of adult crane flies.

Crane flies are often attracted to lights at night and may be seen in their natural environments flying clumsily near streams and ponds and other wet areas. The particularly observant trout fisherman, however, may see another kind of crane fly that is particularly interesting.

The phantom crane fly is much like other crane flies in form and size, but its long legs are conspicuously marked with black and white bands. In addition, the phantom crane fly is such a poor flier that it barely bothers to use its wings at all. Instead, it spreads it legs and floats upon the air currents like a milkweed seed, drifting down the breeze like a banded phantom and making the observer wonder if what he thinks he is seeing is really there.

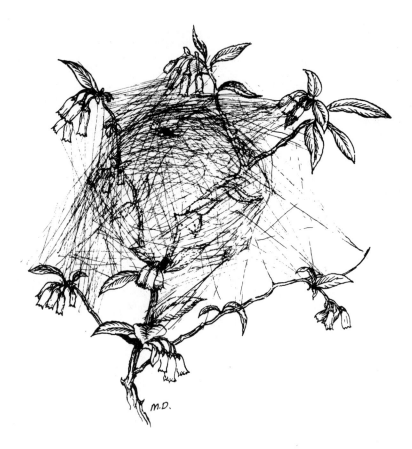

Filmy-Dome and Bowl-and-Doily Spiders

In the spring, at about the time eager trout fishermen are making their ways through the budding woods *en route* to their favorite streams, two closely related spiders are building webs of such exquisite designs that they must not be missed. You need not go out of your way to find them, for I have often seen dozens along a short stretch of railroad track or along a path through the woods that leads down to a favorite pool. Both types of webs sparkle in the sunlight like amazing jewels, yet they are so easily overlooked.

One type of web is called the filmy-dome web and is precisely that. It is made by a tiny spider that hangs under the ceiling of the dome and pulls trapped insects through to the inside. The dome itself can be about four inches across the base and is built in small, woodland shrubs like highbush blueberry.

The other type of web, built by a close relative of the filmy-dome spider, is in the form of a bowl and doily. The bowl is of much the same form and size as the dome, but it is turned over to form a bowl, open side up. About an inch below the bowl is a flat, sheet-like web that is the doily. The bowl-and-doily spider is also only about ¼ of an inch overall and it spends its time on the underside of the bowl, protected from below by the doily. It also builds its webs in the low shrubs of shady woods.

Spring

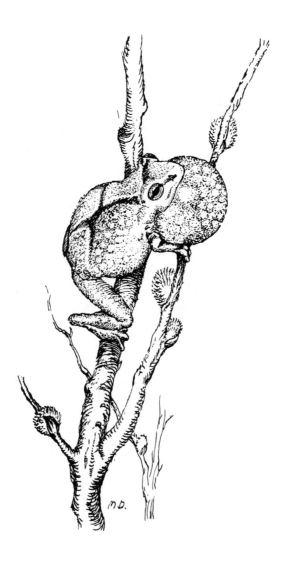

Frog Calls

Nearly every fisherman throughout the country is familiar with the call of the bullfrog. The penetrating "jug-o-rum" is heard on lakes and ponds not only on summer evenings, but often at midday. Another call familiar to most fishermen in the eastern half of the country is the banjo-like "gunk" of the green frog. A similar call is made in the southern tier of eastern states by the bronze frog.

But there are many more frog calls that can be heard in the woods and ponds during the spring and summer. Some are so musical that you will think they could be made only by birds, while others are so mechanical that they seem like the calls of insects.

In early spring, the turkey hunter may hear what sounds like a flock of ducks in a woodland pond. That is the call made by wood frogs, which range across all of Canada, through Alaska, and throughout the northeast quarter of the United States.

The piping call of the spring peepers will be heard from marshes throughout the eastern half of the country. A marsh full of peepers sounds very much like sleigh bells.

A sound like pebbles being clicked together is the call of cricket frogs, found throughout the southern and central parts of the country, while chorus frogs in most states emit a trilled "prrreep" like a fingernail run across the teeth of a comb.

Leopard frogs are common in ponds nearly everywhere, and they emit a loud snore followed by clucks. A similar but less forceful snore is made by the pickerel frog in many central and eastern states.

And perhaps the sweetest, most birdlike trill is the call of the American toad, heard throughout the spring in the shallow ponds of most central and eastern states.

All of these calls are the love songs of the males as they try to attract mates. Listen for them.

Spring

Laurel and Barberry

The turkey hunter will be the most likely sportsman to be in the right place at the right time to investigate the blossoms of the mountain laurel. Barberry is less particular about habitat, not requiring the rocky, upland areas preferred by the mountain laurel. The fisherman, therefore, cutting through an overgrown hedgerow, may have an opportunity to investigate the blossoms of the barberry.

The two plants are not related. The only reason they have been brought together on this page is because both plants make use of a similar, mechanical theme for getting their pollen onto insects.

Look at a blossom of the mountain laurel. It is bowl-shaped with the female part sticking straight out of the center and the ten male parts cocked back into pockets around the sides. When a bee comes in to sip nectar, any laurel pollen she has on her body will immediately touch the central, female part of the blossom. Then, as she fumbles around in the blossom, she will dislodge the spring-like male parts from their pockets and they will spring out and catapult their webby pollen all over her. She'll then take that to the next blossom. Imitate a bee yourself by using a little twig or pine needle, and watch the mechanism work.

The barberry blossom is still more interesting because it seems even more mechanical. It doesn't spring; it moves slowly like a machine. The yellow flower, though smaller, is built similarly to that of the laurel, but with only six male parts. Touch the base of each male part with a pine needle and watch it slowly move in to leave its pollen on the needle. It does the same thing to a bee's tongue and face, and each of the six male parts works independently. In the fall, the barberry bears small, oval, red berries that are edible but as sour as a lemon.

I've known anglers to get so caught up in playing with these blossoms that they almost forgot about fishing. Almost.

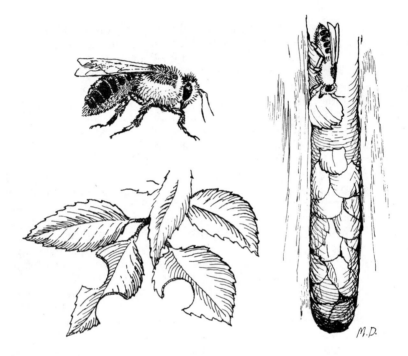

Leaf-Cutter Bees

While you are tramping around in the woods this spring looking for a new trout stream, keep an eye open for leaves that have perfectly round or oval pieces cut out of them. The holes are the work of leaf-cutter bees, and they are made with astonishing precision.

Most kinds of bees do not live in hives. In fact, only honey bees live communally. Other kinds of bees, of which there are many, lead solitary lives, and each female is responsible for her own egglaying and for providing for her young.

The female leaf-cutter bee first finds an old tunnel in dead wood or excavates a new one. Then she cuts several oval-shaped leaf pieces and lines the end of the tunnel with them. Next she packs the end of the tunnel with bee-bread (a mixture of pollen and honey) and lays an egg on it. Then she cuts several round pieces of leaves that are the same diameter as the tunnel and packs them into the hole like a stack of records. Then she cuts more oval pieces of leaves, packs them with bee-bread, lays another egg, and so on until the tunnel is filled.

The eggs hatch and the larvae feed on the bee-bread. When it is gone, they pupate, and then they change into adult bees, each within its little packet in the tunnel. The first egg laid is the first to mature, but it must wait until each of the others has emerged before it can leave the tunnel.

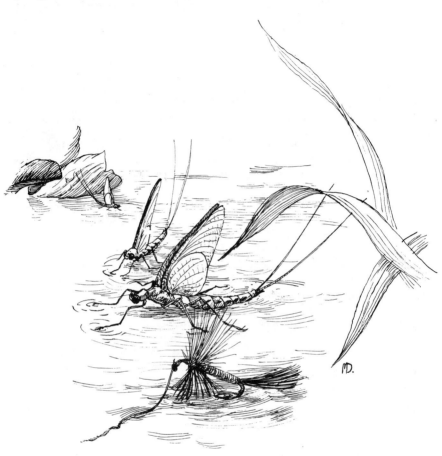

Mayflies

Mayflies used to be what dry fly fishing for trout was all about. "Matching the hatch" referred to mayflies. Quill Gordons, Hendricksons, Cahills, March Browns are all fly fishermen's names for different species of mayflies. Nowadays, other types of aquatic and terrestrial insects play equally important parts in fly fishing, but the mayflies still hold a special place in the tradition of the sport.

Every trout fisherman is familiar with mayflies, and to those who have witnessed a good-sized hatch on a stream, it seems impossible that all other sportsman are not equally familiar with these insects. Yet, because mayflies are so closely associated with aquatic environments, those sportsmen who do little trout fishing may be unaware of the mayfly.

Most of any mayfly's life is spent under water in the nymph stage. Those anglers who fish with nymphs are fishing with imitations of the immature stage of the mayfly. During that stage, the mayfly breathes by means of external gills that are located along both sides of its abdomen. Mayfly nymphs eat mostly decaying vegetable matter and are active little insects that either burrow in the bottom, climb on plants, or swim like little minnows depending on their species. Many remain in the nymph stage for as many as three years.

As adults, however, their lives are rather short and single-minded. Their entire mission is to mate and lay eggs. Adult mayflies do not even eat, and most live only a few days.

Fly fishermen refer to the emergence of the adults from their nymphal form as the "hatch." At such times, enormous numbers of the same species of mayfly emerge from the water as winged adults and float on the surface while their wings prepare for flight. This is the stage that the traditional dry flies are meant to imitate.

But there is one particularly interesting aspect of the lives of mayflies that makes them different from all other insects. Only mayflies molt after they have become winged adults. When they first emerge from their nymphal skins, mayflies are known as duns. Their wings are cloudy, and their body colors are muted. After their unusual molt, their wings become crystal clear, body coloring intensifies, and the insects are ready to mate. Now they are called spinners.

Great clouds of spinners form mating swarms, and the spent insects fall on the water in enormous numbers. That is called a "spinner fall" and the time you should fish with "spentwing" flies.

Spring

Mayfly Midge

Trout fishermen always hope to find themselves in the middle of a mayfly hatch. At such times, enormous clouds of dancing mayflies swarm above the water and mate. The males identify the females by sight and, upon seeing one, grab her from below and mate with her within the swarm.

The angler willing to take a few minutes off from fishing at such a time can observe the mating behavior within a swarm, for the cloud of insects may be only a few inches from his head. He may, in fact, be entirely surrounded by the swarm and had best keep his mouth shut.

During those swarms, the observant angler may notice an insect within the swarm that looks slightly different from the rest. It may have a slightly different color, and it will certainly exhibit a much longer tail. It seems almost to drift through the swarm like a ghost, and in the half-light of dusk, the angler will usually get only a sense of the thing rather than a good look.

That insect is a biting midge that preys upon male mayflies. It has a pair of long, trailing glands that apparently resemble the tails of a female mayfly enough to attract the attentions of a male. When a male mayfly mistakes the midge for a female mayfly and attempts to mate with it, the midge eats the mayfly.

There are usually only a few of these mayfly midges patrolling a mating swarm; so they must be carefully watched for. Very few naturalists, let alone sportsmen, know about them.

Night-Blooming Flowers

As evening approaches, the trout fisherman on some wooded stream in late spring will notice a perceptible increase in the fragrance of the air. He may notice it while he is still on the stream, or as he walks a woodland trail back to his car. If he is enchanted enough by the fragrance, he may seek its source. And if he finds it, he will have found one of the night-blooming flowers.

One of the most common of the night-blooming flowers is the swamp azalea. This plant is a shrub that grows along the banks of streams in wooded areas, and its showy, white blossoms are a common sight to trout fishermen. During the day, the blossoms are open. But if you were to take a moment to sample their fragrance, you would find that there is not much to them—not much, at least, in comparison to the almost overpowering perfume they give off with the approach of evening.

The same is true of the honeysuckles, the evening primrose, night-flowering catchfly, and others. But what is going on here? Why would some flowers want to save their perfumes for the nighttime? It may seem that the purpose is to seduce the fisherman into staying a little longer, but there is more to it than that.

Flowers that bloom and/or become fragrant at night are trying to attract moths. Look at some samples of the various, night-blooming flowers. You will notice that they all have some characteristics in common. They are all fairly deep. An insect must have a long tongue to reach their stores of nectar. A bee would be too small. The internal parts of these flowers are arranged for insects the size and shape of moths. Additionally, all the night-blooming flowers are white, yellow, or light pink. That makes them easier to find at night when even the faintest light makes them seem to glow.

Moths have a wonderful sense of smell, and they can home in on the fragrant blossoms from enormous distances. While dining at the nectar-filled blossoms, they inadvertently cross-pollinate the flowers. All concerned parties come out ahead.

Spring

Pine Pollen

In late spring, the fisherman on pond, stream, or even miles out on open water of the Great Lakes will begin to notice a yellow haze upon the surface of the water. Within a couple of weeks, windrows of the yellow dust will form along shorelines as wind and wave action concentrate the powder to leeward.

As you may have guessed, that yellow powder is pollen. But you may not have realized that all of it, and much more of it that has not fallen upon the water, is from the same plant. That plant is the pine.

Trees, of course, are flowering plants (see "Tree Blossoms"), and pines release more pollen than do most trees. Because pines entrust their pollination solely to the vagueries of the wind and not to the predictable and dependable activities of insects, enormous amounts of pollen are produced to ensure fertilization of the female flowers and the production of cones and seeds.

Pines have separate male and female flowers on each tree. The female flowers are rarely seen, for they are borne on the very tips of the new growth in the highest parts of the tree. The male flowers, however, can be seen along the new growth in the lower parts of the tree where they look like clusters of mulberries.

Once the male pine flowers release their stores of pollen, clouds of the yellow powder can be seen blowing off the trees. The female flowers that receive some of the pollen become mature cones in two years, while male flowers shrivel and fall soon after giving up their pollen.

When the yellow haze starts appearing on the water, keep a close watch above for the pollen clouds.

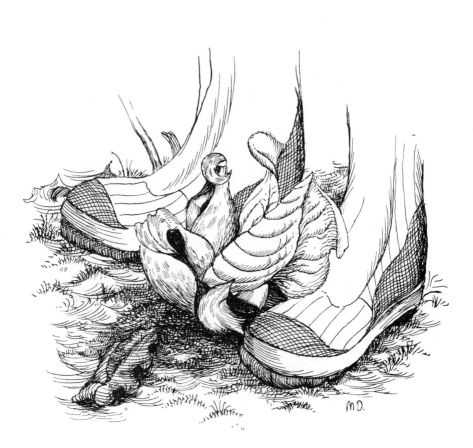

Skunk Cabbage

The very first indications of spring are found in the low, wet places where impatient trout fishermen go prematurely to make sure the stream will still be there on opening day. Those sportsmen will notice the appearance of purplish shoots poking up through the soft mud even while snow covers the streambanks. Most sportsmen realize that those shoots are awakening skunk cabbages and that, in a few days, they will be about three inches tall and will look like conical horns. They know, too, that by late spring and throughout the summer the plants will continue to grow abundant, cabbagey leaves that will be a foot in length and will give off a distinctly disagreeable odor. Hence the name.

But what most sportsmen do not realize is that the little, tentlike horns do not become the leaves. The leaves grow later, after the horns have done their work. The horns are the flowers.

Inside each horn-shaped tent is a thing that looks like a short corncob. It is covered with flowers that have both male and female parts. Bees are attracted to the flowers because, this early in the season, the skunk cabbages provide the only source of pollen around. But the skunk cabbage flowers are not really designed for bees; they are designed for pollination by small flies and gnats, and that's why they stink. Given a choice, a bee will go to a flower that smells nice. Flies are attracted to blossoms that stink.

This ploy is not unique to the skunk cabbage. One species of trillium, or wake-robin, employs the same ruse, and the pretty blossoms of carrion flower so strongly smell of rotting flesh that smelling them will make you gag. Keep a nose out for them.

Sphagnum

If you have ever bought nightcrawlers from a bait shop (and what angler hasn't at one time or another?), or hellgrammites, crayfish, spikes, or any other kind of live bait that had to be kept moist but not wet, these animals were undoubtedly boxed in damp sphagnum.

Sphagnums comprise about forty species of mosses out of about 14,000 total species of mosses. Bogs are built primarily of sphagnum mosses, and "quaking bogs" are actually mats of sphagnum that are reinforced by intertwining roots of other bog plants and are floating on the surface of the water.

When sphagnum dies, decays, settles to the bottom of the bog, and is compressed by the weight of additional material over time, peat is formed. Bricks of peat are the primary fuel in some parts of the world. It takes about a hundred years for a bog to build one foot of peat.

Dried sphagnum (recently living plants as opposed to long-dead peat) and peat are both so highly absorbent that they lend themselves to a great many common uses. Trees and other plants are packed in sphagnum for shipment so that they will retain moisture. Bandages for medical use are made of sphagnum. Virtually any situation in which moisture must be absorbed or retained for long periods of time calls for sphagnum. It is clean, inexpensive, and infinitely reusable. Sphagnum has the remarkable ability to absorb twenty times its own weight in water.

Fishermen should always have a supply on hand. The greatest danger to most soft-bodied, live baits is their drying out. Baits packed in moistened sphagnum will stay cool and damp for hours without getting overly wet. And don't throw the used moss away. You can dry it out and remoisten it indefinitely.

Spittlebugs

When you are on your way to that meadow stream or farm pond surrounded by weedy fields, you will surely notice the small, white, frothy globs on the stems of clovers and grasses. The froth is variously called cow-spit, snake-spit, or frog-spit, depending on the locale. But it is not actually any kind of spit. The froth is made by a small, green insect called the spittlebug that is living within the foam.

It is the immature forms that live in the spittle, and you will want to take a closer look at one of them. Just carefully clear away the foam in one of those masses, and you will find the green, slightly frog-shaped nymph holding onto the plant's stem.

To create the foam (and this is something you can watch if you have the time), the young insect sucks up a flow of plant juice through its beak-like mouth. some of the juice provides the spittlebug with nourishment, but the large amount of excess just keeps going right through the nymph's system and out of its anus. Then it pours down over the insect and is blown full of air from the holes in the nymph's sides, causing it to foam up.

The foam keeps the nymph from drying-out in the hot, meadow sun and provides protection from enemies.

There are also dark-colored spittlebug nymphs that feed on the twigs of pines. When you are passing through a stand of pines to get to a stream or while on a turkey hunt, watch for these dark-colored spittlebugs as well. Excess juice, dripping from above, may fool you into thinking it's raining.

Spittlebug adults look like husky, brown leafhoppers. They spend their time feeding inconspicuously on plant juices and don't make spittle. They are hard to find because they don't have the spittle to call attention to themselves.

Spring

Springtails

The summer fisherman and the winter hunter are equally likely to encounter springtails. But the fisherman will probably call them water-fleas, and the hunter will know them as snow-fleas.

When you are fishing a quiet cove, dotted with lilypads in midsummer, you may notice upon the pads, and even upon the surface of the water itself, a charcoal-gray mass. Look closely, and you will find that the mass is made up of myriad tiny gray creatures that spring away like fleas when you try to touch them.

Each of those creatures has a forked appendage on the rear of its abdomen that is folded forward under its body and is held there under tension by a clip-like structure. When the clip lets go, the forked appendage springs down and back, and the little springtail is catapulted a comparatively great distance.

On sunny days in the winter, when warm microclimates form near the bases of rocks and trees, it is common to find sooty patches on the snow. On closer inspection, those turn out, again, to be a mass of springtails that have come up from the leaf-litter to enjoy the warmth and perhaps to feed on algae on the surface of the snow.

There are over 300 different species of springtails in North America inhabiting a great variety of environments.

Spring

Stoneflies

Stoneflies, along with mayflies and caddisflies, are one of the most important aquatic insects to fly fishermen. Both the adults and the immature nymphs are imitated by fly tiers and provide excellent fishing under the right circumstances.

The nymphs of stoneflies are often confused with the nymphs of mayflies. Stonefly nymphs, however, have long antennae, only two tails, and usually have two pairs of wing pads on their backs. They also lack any feathery gills along the sides of their abdomens. Mayfly nymphs lack long antennae, often have three tails but only one pair of wing pads, and usually display gills along their abdomen.

Like mayflies, stoneflies spend their immaturity under water and pass directly to the adult stage without going through a pupal stage. When ready to emerge as an adult, the stonefly nymph climbs out of the water onto a rock, and then emerges as a winged adult. Unlike the mayflies, stonefly adults spend almost no time on the water.

Nor do stoneflies mate in swarms. Mating takes place on land with individuals finding each other by sight or by sound. Some species of stoneflies signal the other sex by beating their bodies against a hard surface and drumming to each other. Egg-laying takes place by the females running over the surface of the water and dipping their abdomens below the surface. Dry fly imitations of the adults are effective when they mimic that behavior.

Adult stoneflies are long and slender insects that hold their wings folded flat over their backs when at rest. When in flight, they can easily be mistaken for either mayflies or caddisflies. Unlike those insects, though, adult stoneflies can be found in the dead of winter crawling upon the surface of the snow near streams.

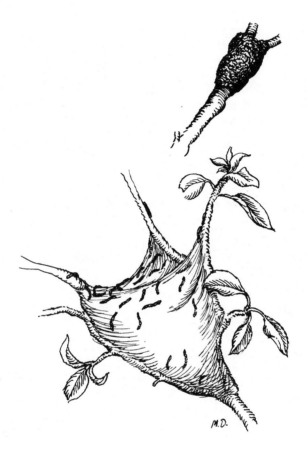

Tent Caterpillars

Any sportsman walking through the woods in the spring is sure to notice the white webbing in the crotches of young cherry and apple trees. They are the tents of colonies of tent caterpillars—the larvae of a specific kind of moth—and they are found only in the spring. They are often confused with a similar structure found in the fall, but that is something else (see "Fall Webworms"). If it is in spring, it must be tent caterpillars.

During the winter, the egg masses of tent caterpillars can be found on the branches of cherry and apple trees, and when they hatch in the spring, the hundreds of tiny caterpillars immediately begin building their communal tent. During the growth stage of the larvae, the tent is continually being enlarged. Silk is added in continuous sheets that are separated somewhat from the layer within. This not only allows the caterpillars to move between the layers, but the construction serves as a sort of greenhouse, trapping heat on sunny but cold days. Temperatures have been found to be twice as high inside the tent as outside.

Three times each day—early morning, noon, and evening—the caterpillars leave the tent to feed on the leaves of the tree in which the tent is built. They each lay down a trail of silk that eventually becomes plainly visible to the observer. Encoded in the silk trails are messages about the availability of food. Outgoing caterpillars can follow the most promising trails laid down by returning larvae.

By early summer, the larvae leave the tent to pupate. Each goes its separate way, weaves a powdery, tough cocoon in some protected place and, by midsummer, emerges as an adult moth. After mating, the females lay their eggs on the right trees and cover them with a dark brown, foamy lacquer that dries into the tough cases found in winter. Then the adults die.

If you are not too squeamish, poke your finger into the silk of one of those tents. You're sure to be impressed by its strength.

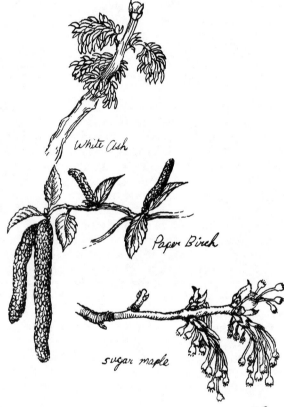

White Ash

Paper Birch

sugar maple

M.D.

Tree Blossoms

The early-season trout fisherman will be among the first to notice the coming of spring. Down in the thawing wetlands and creek edges, green things begin to happen. Trees, too, on south-facing hillsides, take on a pastel hue as buds begin to swell and open. Soon there is definite growth on the trees, and a wide panorama of the woodlands from a good vantage point reveals a landscape very much like the colorful variety of autumn, but much less brilliant, much more subdued. All the colors are there, though—reds, oranges, yellows, and greens. Most observers think they are the colors of the emerging leaves. Very few realize they are the colors of flowers.

All trees have flowers, though it is one of the best kept secrets of nature. Everyone is, of course, familiar with the flowers of apple, cherry, magnolia, and dogwood trees, for those flowers are showy and obvious. But the subtle, smoky hues of the spring trees are owed to the blossoms of willows, poplars, elms, maples, and birches.

Flowers like the showy blossoms of the apples have both male and female parts within the same blossom. So do the flowers of the elms, basswoods and tulip tree, though the flowers of the elms are very inconspicuous and appear early, well before the leaves.

Trees like maples, birches, oaks, hickories, walnuts, and pines bear separate male and female flowers with both types of flowers on the same tree.

The ashes, willows, and poplars have separate male and female trees. The male trees produce only male flowers, and the female trees produce only female flowers. That's why only some ashes produce seeds. Those are the female trees.

Look closer at those early spring trees. Their flowers are among the first of the year, often appearing well before their leaves.

Spring

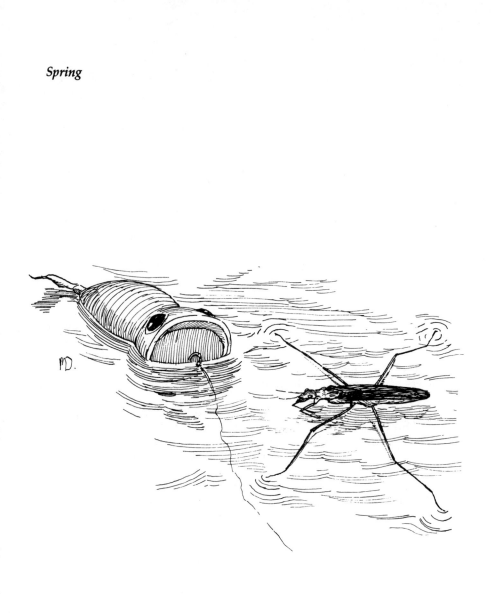

Water Striders

Stream fishermen, lake fishermen, and even saltwater fishermen are equally likely to see water striders, for these insects inhabit all types of aquatic environments including the open ocean. Water striders are those long-legged insects that skate upon the surface and appear to have only four legs. They actually have six, however, as do all insects, but their front pair is short and held beneath the head. Those front legs are for capturing prey.

The water strider is a predator, feeding on other insects on the surface of the water. In some respects, the water strider uses the water's surface film much as a spider uses a web. Not only do insects get stuck in the film, but vibrations made by a trapped insect are transmitted to the water strider by the surface film. Thus, the strider can locate trapped insects, grab them with its front legs, pierce them with its beak, and suck out their juices.

Water striders also use the surface film to communicate with each other. By drumming upon the surface of the water with its middle pair of legs, the male water striders send out vibrations that serve a dual purpose. First, they attract females for mating, indicating that the male has found a good place for the females to lay eggs and inviting them to it. Secondly, it warns other males that they will be attacked if they venture too close to the territory claimed by that male. After mating takes place, the female lays her eggs upon the piece of wood or plant that the male has claimed.

Adult water striders may be fully winged, have small wings, or have no wings at all. All three forms may be found in the same population.

Although water striders are extremely common, and most trout streams have an abundant population of them, I have yet to see one be eaten by a fish. In fact, I have had trout take a fly that I thought was an imitation of a water strider while ignoring the real things. Apparently, "skaters"—long hackles wound around a short-shanked hook—are not imitations of water striders but of something else that trout like better than striders: crane flies.

I wonder if anyone has ever seen a trout eat a water strider.

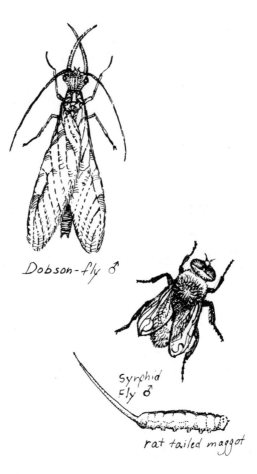

Dobson-fly ♂

Syrphid
Fly ♂

rat tailed maggot

What's What in Live Baits

Fishermen who use live bait may collect or buy a variety of creatures that are commonly used to catch fish. Some of those baits are well known to everyone, whether sportsman or not, and present no mystery as to how they fit into the general scheme of things. Frogs are frogs; crickets are crickets; shiners are shiners; crayfish are crayfish; and, of course, worms are worms.

But they are a few other creatures commonly sold as bait that, were they allowed to reach their natural maturity, would grow up to be insects that would surely surprise the angler.

Smallmouth bass fishermen will be familiar with hellgrammites or dobsons. They are themselves rather evil-looking, aquatic larvae with biting jaws. When mature, hellgrammites become large, soft-bodied, night-flying insects called dobsonflies that can reach a length of four inches. Male dobsonflies have enormous, caliper-like jaws that can be half as long as the body. The adults are common, but because they rarely fly during the day, they are not often seen.

Another common bait sold in some parts of the country is the outsized nymph of a mayfly. The adults of the creamy-yellow mayflies are known in most places as the Michigan caddis, even though they are not caddisflies.

Mousies are also a popular bait. A mousie is a rattailed maggot that is so named because it possesses an extensible breathing tube that, when extended, resembles the tail of a rat or mouse. When mature, mousies become a type of flower fly called syrphids. Most syrphids look like houseflies disguised as bees. They eat pollen and are protected from predators by their black and yellow markings, which make them look as though they sting. They don't. But that kind of mimicry is fairly common among insects.

The well-known catalpaworm becomes a well camouflaged, brown, sphinx moth with a wingspread of about 3 ½ inches. Sphinx moths are also called hawkmoths for their narrow wings and swooping flight.

Another common bait sold in some parts of the country is the outsized nymph of a mayfly. The adults of the creamy-yellow mayflies are known in most places as the Michigan caddis even though they are not caddisflies.

Woodcock

Woodcock hunters are probably wondering why I have placed the woodcock in the spring section when the bird is hunted in the fall. The answer is that I am not writing about the woodcock for the hunter. I am writing about woodcock for the fisherman, who is most likely to encounter woodcock in the spring.

By early April, around opening day of the trout season in most places, the woodcock have returned North to their nesting grounds, and the males make themselves apparent to both the female woodcock and trout fishermen. Just about the time that the angler is thinking about quitting the stream for lack of light, the male woodcock begins his mating flight.

The flights take place in special clearings, usually in the woods, in meadows, or near streams. The male flies to the center of the clearing and stands quietly for a few moments. Then he suddenly flies into the air and climbs steadily to a height of over two hundred feet, all the while emitting a whistling or twittering sound. At the apex of the ascent, the sound changes to a more melodious song that is sung as the bird drops on fluttering wings. Then it lands near the spot it took off from and emits a buzzy "peenting" call on the ground. Each of those flights lasts about a minute and is repeated every five minutes or so. Ultimately, the display causes a female to appear in the clearing, and the pair mate.

The woodcock eats earthworms, which it seeks in moist areas by probing in the mud with its long bill. The upper mandible of the woodcock's bill is hinged near its tip so that the bird can use the bill as a forceps once a worm is located. Another adaptation to its feeding habits is the set of its eyes, which seem to be much too far back on its head. That placement of the eyes, however, allows the bird to be aware of the approach of danger even while its bill is deep in the mud.

Woodcock are active only very early in the morning and late in the evening, times of day when the light level is extremely low but not dark. Birds and animals that are active at those times are called crepuscular, as opposed to diurnal (active in daylight) or nocturnal (active at night).

Because of the low light level when the male woodcock make their mating flights, the sportsman is more likely to hear than see them. But if you direct your gaze toward the sound, you may be lucky enough to catch the small, spiralling silhouette against the fading sky.

Summer

Summer

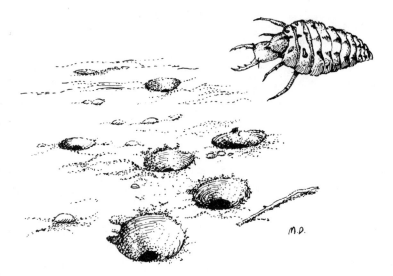

Ant-Lions

Fishing in the rain can be remarkably rewarding. But every so often a summer cloudburst comes along that causes even the most rugged fisherman to get off the stream and take shelter beneath the eaves of an old barn or within the sheltering boughs of an evergreen. In such protected places can often be found the traps of the ant-lions.

Ant-lions in their adult forms are harmless-looking, delicate insects that resemble dragonflies. But in their larval stages, they are fat, little, grublike creatures that look like half-inch-long lice with enormous jaws. Those predatory larvae feed on ants and other small insects, and they build traps to catch them.

The ant-lions build their traps in dry, dusty soil. By moving backwards in a tight spiral and flicking upwards with its head, the larva causes a funnel-shaped pit to be formed with itself at the bottom. When an ant ventures over the brink of the trap, the shifting walls cause it to fall into the waiting jaws of the ant-lion.

Ant-lions tend to build their traps in colonies. If you are fortunate enough to come upon such a colony, you can wait out the rain by gently tickling the sides of the funnels with a pine needle or a blade of grass. That will usually elicit a lot of head-flicking from the owners.

Ant-lion larvae are sometimes known as doodlebugs.

Summer

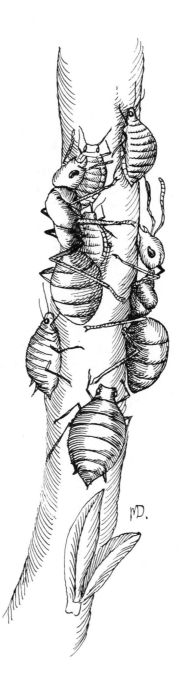

Aphids

Aphids clustered upon the new growth of succulent meadow or streamside plants should be a familiar sight to most sportsmen. The sight may be so familiar, in fact, that little notice has been given to it, but aphids are truly unusual insects with extraordinary life cycles.

In the spring or early summer, eggs that were laid last fall hatch. Every single aphid that hatches out of those eggs is a wingless female. Those females poke their beaks into the growing part of the plant upon which they feed and suck out the sap. They grow quickly on the rich nutriment and give birth to live young. No mating takes place because there are no males to mate with anyway. The original females, called "stem mothers," just go ahead and give birth to more wingless females who eventually give birth to more wingless females themselves. Before long, as you can well imagine, the plant gets pretty crowded with aphids.

The overcrowding sets off a new development. Females with wings start to be born. These are capable of flying to new plants, which are sometimes the same kind of plant as before, or an entirely different species of plant known as the "alternate host." In any case, the winged females migrate to the new plant and commence giving birth to more live, wingless females.

Towards fall, eggs must be laid that can overwinter and produce next summer's stem mothers. Eggs can only be produced sexually, and the females begin giving birth to both males and females. Those males and females mate, and the females lay eggs on the proper plants—the original host plants, not the alternate hosts.

Beyond this almost unbelievable life history, aphids also have an extraordinary relationship with ants. In the process of feeding on plant sap, excess sap is expelled by each aphid through the tip of its abdomen. Close observation will easily reveal those tiny drops of sap. Ants love the sugary liquid, and a mutually beneficial alliance exists between the insects. The aphids provide the ants with "honeydew," while the ants protect the otherwise defenseless aphids from a variety of enemies.

There's certainly a lot more to those ubiquitous aphids than you ever imagined, isn't there?

Summer

Backswimmers and Water Boatmen

Although ice fishermen in some areas may catch an occasional glimpse of these insects throughout the winter, the summer fisherman, sitting quietly in his boat in some weedy cove, will have the greatest opportunity to observe backswimmers and water boatmen.

Because both types of insects have sunflower seed-shaped bodies and extra-long, hind swimming legs, they are often confused. Worse yet, you may not even realize that there are two different kinds of insects here.

The backswimmer really resembles a rowboat with oars extended out both sides. As its name implies, it swims on its back, which is keeled for maneuverability. Most often you'll spot backswimmers hanging at a 45 degree angle, head down, from the underside of the surface film in quiet waters. In such a pose, they may be either refilling their oxygen supply or feeling for prey, for it is believed that, like a spider on its web, the hairs on the legs of backswimmers can detect vibrations in the surface film that are made by potential prey. Prey may consist of other insects, small fish, and tadpoles. By injecting digestive juices into its captives through its beak, the backswimmer predigests its food, sucking out the "soup" later. Needless to say, carelessly handled backswimmers can inflict a bite you will not soon forget.

Water boatmen swim right-side-up. Their mouths are very different from the beaks of most bugs (the order of insects to which both the water boatmen and the backswimmers belong). Water boatmen, therefore, are not restricted to sucking juices and can grind plant material, animal matter and detritus. Yet, they don't bite.

You have probably noticed that most animals, birds, fish, and insects are darker above and lighter below. The same is true with water boatmen. But look at the backswimmers you find. They are lighter on their backs than on their undersides because they swim upside-down.

Summer

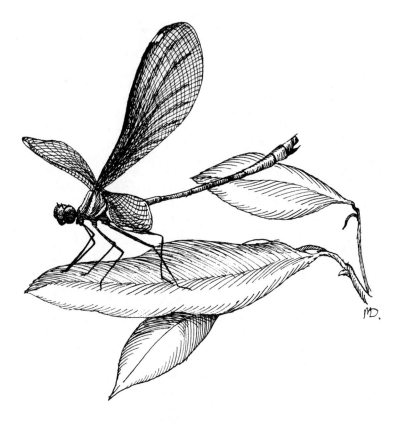

Black-Winged Damselflies

Trout fishermen more than anyone else will have the opportunity of seeing the black-winged damselflies. In fact, they can hardly help but see them. So common are the black-winged damselflies that sportsmen walking through the woods in summer or fishing along a stream will notice dozens of the beautiful insects with their metallic, green bodies and black, fluttering wings flying and perching throughout the area. Though the insects seen in the woods are the same as the insects along the stream, they are not engaged in the same activities.

Most noticeable of the black-winged damselflies—the ones with the bright green, metallic bodies and black wings—are the males. The females are mostly brown with a white spot at the front tip of each wing. Naturally the duller coloring of the females makes them less conspicuous, but watch for them. They will be important to your understanding of the males' activities.

The black-winged damselflies you see well back in the woods, away from the stream, are feeding. They are in the woods to catch a meal. They do that by perching on a branch or leaf, often near a patch of sunlight. When a prey insect such as a mosquito or midge flies through the sunlit patch, it shows up well against the relatively darker background of the unlit woods. The damselfly spots it right away, flies out from its perch, and scoops it up in the basket formed by its hairy legs. Then it takes it back to its perch and eats it.

Those black-winged damselflies along the stream are engaged in a different activity—mating. The males are defending specific, small territories that they protect from the intrusion of other males. A male's territory usually consists of an area of water from which a few plants emerge, providing both a perch for the male and submerged stems upon which the female can lay her eggs. If you see a male perched on a plant with its wings spread straight out like an airplane and its abdomen raised, you are seeing a display meant to drive other males out of the territory. But if you see a male with its back wings spread out straight while its front wings are held pointing upwards, you are seeing a display that is directed towards a female in the area. He is inviting her to mate, and if she responds favorably, she will soon be laying her eggs on the submerged plant stems in the male's territory.

Summer

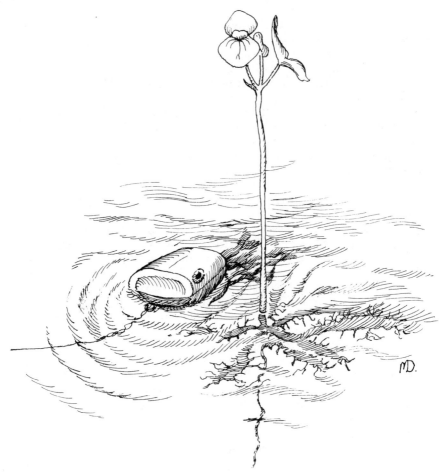

Bladderwort

Fishermen throughout the country will want to watch for a particular aquatic plant while they are fishing. The plant makes itself apparent by putting forth a very pretty, pealike flower that is yellow in some species and purple in others. While the flower is busy attracting pollinators above the surface, the rest of the plant, which is submerged, is busy eating tiny, aquatic animals.

This plant is called the bladderwort, and it is extremely common in lakes and ponds, often growing within beds of other aquatic weeds, such as coontail and lilies. Bladderwort has no roots. It floats just below the surface where its filamentous leaves (which look like roots) spread out horizontally and are kept afloat by tiny bladders. The bladders are scattered throughout the leaves and are about the size of a pin-head.

But the bladders serve yet another purpose. They are actually tiny traps with clever and intricate mechanisms. Each bladder is like a tiny purse with a slit-like opening lined with hairs. When one of the minute water creatures, like a water flea, swims near a bladder and touches one of the hairs, the bladder inflates, drawing water, the flea, and any other nearby creatures inside. Once it draws its captives in, the bladder closes, trapping and digesting its prey.

Next time you are fishing a lure near the surface, and you bring a mess of weeds back with it, check to see if you have caught some bladderwort. You may want to give the plant a closer look (perhaps even with a hand lens) before tossing it back. Watch for the emergent yellow or purple flowers. They are small, but out on a lake, any flower at all is conspicuous.

Summer

Carrion Beetles

Carrion beetles are husky, black beetles, about an inch in length, with red markings. They can be observed by any sportsman who has the stomach for keeping an eye on the bodies of small, dead animals. That, admittedly, may not sound like a particularly pleasant pursuit, but carrion beetles are worth watching, nonetheless.

The beetles specialize in small corpses. Mice, snakes, fish, and small birds are just the right size. Usually operating at night, a carrion beetle locates a dead animal by the extraordinary sense of smell in its knobbed antennae. The corpse will provide food for the beetle and, more importantly, for the beetle's offspring. What is so noteworthy about this scenario is that in order for the egglaying and raising of the young to occur, the beetle, with the help of its mate, must first bury the dead animal completely, often to a depth of several inches.

If the corpse is on suitable ground, the beetles dig beneath it, removing earth until the animal is well below ground level. Then they push earth on top of the body, and it is buried. Often, though, the corpse is not on suitable ground and must be moved. While one beetle prepares the ground several inches away, its mate begins heaving the body towards the burial site until both beetles can begin undermining and burying it. We are talking here of two inch-long insects moving and completely burying a relatively enormous animal within a few hours. This is a remarkable feat of strength and tenacity. It's like you and your spouse moving a dead elephant several feet and then digging a hole under it until it is buried.

In addition, carrion beetles display a highly unusual trait for an insect. They actually stay below ground and feed their young until the larvae are ready to pupate. Very few non-social insects care for their offspring.

Needless to say, the carrion beetles perform an important service in the process of recycling dead matter. If you come upon a dead bird or animal in your wanderings, gently move it with a stick to see if there are any carrion beetles at work under it. A few minutes' observation will be worth your while.

Summer

Cicadas

One of the most common sounds heard by fishermen anywhere in the country is the call of the cicada. The prolonged, buzzing call heard in the dog-days of summer has contributed to the insect's local names of "heat-bug" and "dog-day harvest fly." The sound, like a matchbox full of sand being shaken so fast that all the beats run together, is produced by a two-inch long bug that is closely related to aphids and spittlebugs. Unlike grasshoppers and crickets, which produce their sounds externally by rubbing wings and/or legs against each other, the male cicada's song is produced entirely internally by vibrating membranes. A large part of its body is hollow to act as a sounding chamber and to amplify the sound.

Mating is, of course, the purpose of the song, and females can be attracted from long distances. The females then lay their eggs in the twigs of trees, and the hatchling nymphs drop down to the ground where they burrow into the earth and feed on roots for anywhere from one to seventeen years, depending on their species. The seventeen-year-locust of the North and the thirteen-year-locust of the South are both species of cicadas. But there are adult cicadas of many species emerging and singing every year.

After it has spent its proper time underground, the nymph digs up to the surface, climbs a little way up a tree trunk, and a winged adult crawls out of the split, nymphal skin. The discarded shells can be found on trees throughout the summer.

Every once in a while, you may be sitting in your boat, and you'll notice that some cicada has ended his song very abruptly, without letting it wind down in the usual decrescendo. That cicada has probably been grabbed by a female cicada-killer wasp. And that cicada's singing days are over (see "Solitary Wasps").

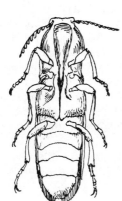
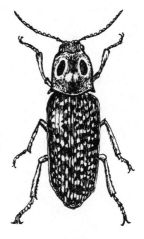

Click Beetles

The fisherman spending the night in camp—whether in a tent, cabin, or lodge—is the most likely sportsman to meet the click beetle, for it is an insect that is often attracted to lights at night (see also "Night Insects"). But meetings with the click beetle are by no means limited to nighttime. It's difficult to tell you where to go to find them because they can be just about anywhere. The best idea is simply to become familiar with what a click beetle looks like so that when you do run across one, you can take advantage of the occasion.

Many species of click beetles range in size from two inches to a fraction of an inch. Most are brownish, slender, shiny, and smooth. They will not bite nor harm you in any way when you handle them. And handle them you should.

The click beetles of all species have a remarkable mechanism that has earned them a variety of local names including "spring beetles," "snapping bugs," and "skipjacks." Because they have a tendency to fold up their legs and fall off their perches when disturbed, they need some mechanism for righting themselves if they land on the ground on their backs. A clip and groove on their undersides provide that mechanism by snapping together with such force that it sends the beetle popping up into the air, sometimes several inches, and producing an audible click. If the beetle doesn't land right-side-up, it tries again.

If you turn a click beetle over on its back, you will be treated to that performance every time.

The larvae of click beetles are called wireworms because of their hard, thin appearance. Some species are found in decayed wood, and some are found underground where they eat roots, occasionally seriously damaging crops like carrots and potatoes. The larvae don't click.

The adult click beetles, though, will provide you with amusement for the rest of your outdoors life.

Donacia Beetles

Most fishermen realize the necessity of letting a surface lure sit quietly for as long as possible. But often it is difficult to summon that kind of patience in one's eagerness for a strike. Perhaps using some of that waiting-time to look for donacia beetles will help.

Donacia beetles are beautiful, bronzy, metallic insects about ⅓ of an inch long that eat leaves. You will notice by midsummer, that nearly all the lilypads have irregular, brown-edged holes in them. Many of those are made by adult donacia beetles. Some of the holes simply represent meals, but some are more interesting. Turn over a couple of pads and look at their undersides. If you are lucky, you will find a ring of tiny eggs around the edge of the hole. The female beetle chews a hole in the pad from above, inserts the tip of her abdomen through the hole and into the water, and lays a batch of eggs that stick to the underside of the pad.

When the eggs hatch into little grubs, the larvae bore into the underwater stems of the lilies, feeding on the plant's tissues while breathing the air that is trapped inside the stem. This air keeps the leaves afloat.

Once the larvae become adult beetles, they live entirely above the water.

Okay. Flick the lure. If you don't get a strike, leave it alone and look for some more eggs.

Dragonflies

Next time you are out in a boat, sitting in a quiet cove and trying to kill fifteen seconds before twitching your surface lure, spend some of those seconds watching dragonflies. Dragonflies are fascinating insects with some highly complex behaviors. They even defend specific territories.

Watch one particular dragonfly. You will usually first spot it perched on a reed-head, or a cattail, or just sitting on a lily-pad. That perch is probably near the center of its territory. Soon it will dart out and grab another insect (often that will be a mosquito or a midge too small for you to see). It may leave its perch to chase away another dragonfly that has entered its territory. Or, if you cast a fly, bass bug, or even a small plug near it, the dragonfly may dart out to investigate that. Almost always it will return to the same perch it just left, or at least one very near it. If you watch long enough, you can even figure out the limits and shape of its territory.

Often you will see two dragonflies flying in tandem. That is a mating pair. The male dragonfly is in front, and he is holding the female behind her head with grasping appendages on the tip of his abdomen. While flying in that position, the female will curl her abdomen under and forward until its tip comes in contact with the second segment of the male's abdomen. That is where his penis is, and sperm will be transferred to the female during flight. Soon after, the male will release his grip on the female, and she will go off and lay eggs by dipping the tip of her abdomen just under the surface of the water.

Female dragonflies, as well as the females of other aquatic insects including mayflies, apparently recognize bodies of water suitable for egglaying by the reflectivity of their surfaces. It is not uncommon, therefore, to see those females lay their eggs on the hoods and roofs of cars.

Dragonfly Larvae

Anglers fishing a quiet backwater may notice what appears to be a large insect hugging an emergent plant stem. On closer examination, the insect will prove to be merely a shed skin, still clinging to the stem. That shed skin probably belonged, recently, to one of the large dragonflies cruising the cove you are fishing.

As perfectly adapted to aerial flight as those adult dragonflies obviously are, their entire immaturity was spent under water where, believe it or not, they were equally well adapted to their environment.

Immature dragonflies are called nymphs or naiads. They are entirely aquatic and breathe through internal gills. They have long legs for walking along the bottoms of lakes and streams, and for clinging to plants. Additionally, they are able to move at a pretty good clip by jet propulsion. They simply take in a quantity of water through their anus and then squirt it back out again. The jet propulsion is generally used for escape rather than for attack. Attack involves yet another neat trick.

Dragonfly larvae are ferocious predators that eat other insects, young fish, tadpoles, and just about anything they can catch and subdue, including each other. Their weapon is an extensible lip. Picture having, in place of your chin and lower jaw, another arm attached at its shoulder to your upper jaw. Normally, you would hold it against your chest, bent at the elbow, with your hand covering your mouth. But if you saw something you wanted to grab, like a hamburger, you could extend your jaw/arm with lightning speed, grab the burger with your hand, retract your jaw/arm again, and have the morsel in your mouth in a flash. That's what dragonfly larvae do.

The nymphs live underwater from one to three years, depending on their species. Some, the ones that become the largest dragonflies, grow to a pretty good size—some over two inches. When the nymphs are fully grown, they crawl up a plant stem until they are above the surface of the water. The nymphal skin splits open, and the winged adult emerges. There is no pupal stage. The skins you find hugging the plant stems are a perfect representation of how the nymphs look. You can even get a good look at that extensible lip.

Summer

Fireflies

Night fishing is usually a highly productive enterprise. Often, good stretches of trout streams run through open meadows near the edges of woods. Fishing such a stretch on a midsummer's night will put the sportsman in a perfect position to observe fireflies.

First, you should realize that there are several different species out there. With that in mind, you will begin to notice that all the flashes made by the fireflies are not alike, nor are they from the same areas of the air. In fact, with careful observation, you should identify several different flash-patterns, for each species has a unique flash and a pre-ferred habitat from which it flashes.

The flashing is for mating. For the most part, fireflies that signal while flying are males. The females flash primarily from the ground or from perches on low plants. Some females have no wings.

Males and females of the same species find each other by exchanging the correct flash-pattern. The flying male signals and watches for the answering signal from a female below. When he gets the right signal, he lands and mates with the female. Males usually mate many times while females mate only once.

Some females, after they have mated with a male of their own species, change their flash-pattern and attract males of other species. When they lure one in, they eat him.

Keep an eye out for the different codes. Variations occur in the number of flashes per second, the number of flashes in a set, shapes of streaks, color, height above ground, habitat, and time of night.

By imitating the patterns with your penlight held close to the ground, you can actually get the males to come right to you.

Fragrant Leaves

Few sportsmen are aware of the various fragrances that are hidden in the leaves of a number of common plants. Like the perfumes of flowers, leaf fragrances are distinct from each other, and the sportsman with a discerning nose can learn to distinguish amongst them. It is not quite so easy to explain their purpose in the life of a plant. Perhaps the plant uses coincidental odors of chemicals in their leaves as natural insect repellents. Or it may be something far more complicated that we have not even begun to imagine. We do know that some plants are pleasingly fragrant, while others just smell like leaves.

Surfcasters along the Atlantic Coast will be familiar with bayberry, a shrub with both fragrant leaves and fragrant, waxy berries from which bayberry candles are made. Its close relative, sweet gale, is similarly fragrant and grows in peaty areas along the shores of lakes and bogs.

Sweet fern, which is actually a low shrub and not a fern at all, grows in waste places and disturbed areas. Continuous groves of the plant are often seen along roadsides where the hot sun causes their fragrance to fill the air.

Sassafras and its close relative, spicebush, grow in moist, woodland environments, often near the banks of streams. Both of these grove-forming plants have delightfully fragrant leaves. In the South, the crushed and dried leaves of sassafras is a common additive to stews and is called "gumbo." The roots of sassafras are also fragrant. This is the source of the flavoring for root beer.

There are more fragrant plants than we have space for. Many of them can be used to make refreshing teas. Most are just nice to smell. Handfuls of the fresh leaves can be placed under the straps of backpacks or creels so that they will be crushed and give off their aromas as you walk. Make a point of rubbing the leaves of plants to see if they are fragrant. Very few plants are poisonous to the touch, and if you learn what those look like, you can safely touch all others. Most of us don't use our noses enough.

A list of a few more fragrant shrubs and wildflowers are as follows: fragrant sumac; sweetshrub; pennyroyal; catnip, and other mints; wintergreen; yarrow; some goldenrods; sweetflag; Labrador tea; pineapple weed; and don't forget the inner bark of black birch.

Kingbirds

Fishermen in most parts of the country have plenty of opportunity to see kingbirds at work. We are talking about kingbirds here—a gray bird with a white band on the tip of its tail that catches flies—not to be confused with kingfishers, which are blue and catch fish. The kingbird is of interest because it is so conspicuously aggressive. It's difficult to fish a lake near a nesting pair of kingbirds without noticing their goings-on.

Early in the season, around May in the North, the kingbirds arrive at their nesting sites. They make themselves obvious right away. The males are aggressive even to their own potential mates at this stage of the game, but they manage to get along just enough to mate. Then, while she is building the nest and brooding the eggs, the female herself becomes aggressive. She drives the male away whenever she catches him too close to the nest. Finally the eggs hatch, and things become a good deal more copacetic between the pair as they share in the prodigious task of gathering food for the growing young.

Even at this relatively peaceful stage in their relationship the kingbirds will be apparent to the sportsman, for each time the male and female meet after a separation of any length, they go through a conspicuous display involving a great deal of wing-fluttering and chittering.

Most impressive of all, though, is the male's aggressive behavior towards crows, owls, and hawks. The relatively small kingbird will unhesitatingly pursue any of those larger predators and will badger it until it leaves the kingbird's territory. Curiously, the kingbird perceives its territory as extending straight up for a hundred feet or so, and he will attack a hawk that appears as a mere speck against the sky. Watch particularly for this reaction, for while returning to its perch from a great height, the kingbird will often perform a spectacular tumbling fall through the air.

Lacewings

Lacewings should be familiar to many sportsmen, though not necessarily by that name. Some may know the insect by the name "golden-eye," and some may know it as "stink-fly." In any case, we are talking about a beautiful, delicate, pale green insect with lacy wings. It is about an inch long with gold eyes, and it emits a rather disgusting odor when handled. All its common names, therefore, apply very well.

Lacewings are in the same order of insects as ant-lions and dobson-flies. Their larvae are called aphis lions. The name indicates their favorite prey and suggests where they are likely to be found.

Look for plants that have a large population of aphids feeding upon their juices. Two kinds of insects will be seeking those plants for the purpose of laying their eggs in the midst of an abundant food supply for their offspring: the lady bird beetle and the lacewing. Both insects have larvae that have insatiable appetites for aphids.

Lacewing larvae—the aphis lions—are such voracious predators that the female lacewing must take special precautions against the first-hatched larvae eating the unhatched eggs. So, before she lays an egg, the female lacewing places a drop of sticky liquid on the surface of a leaf. The liquid is excreted from the tip of her abdomen and is immediately drawn out into a half-inch-long thread. Upon the thread's sticky tip she secures an egg. Thus, she produces a batch of eggs with each perched upon its own stalk. When the hungry little larvae hatch, they find it considerably easier to catch one of the abundant aphids than to climb up a neighboring stalk to eat an egg.

The stalked eggs and the aphis lions are easy to find, and the delicate, beautifully colored adults are worth a close look as well. Note the astonishing golden eyes, and take a quick whiff of the odor given off by the insect. It is not likely to send you off on a gagging fit. Rather, it is another of those items to store in your mental file of natural perfumes.

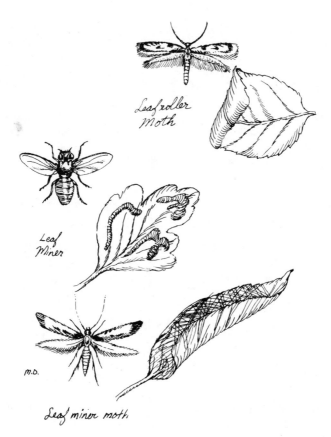

Leafroller
Moth

Leaf
Miner

m.d.

Leaf miner moth.

Leaf Homes

On his way through the woods to a lake or stream in the spring, the fisherman may be struck by the flawlessness of the newly emerging leaves. It is the lack of damage by insects that is conspicuous, for it doesn't take long for the insect hordes to get down to their missions in life—eating and mating. And the diets of a good percentage of insects consist of leaves. By midsummer the leaves of most plants are showing the strain of that onslaught.

Because many of the eaters of leaves are small insects that are prime targets for predators and parasites, many of them have evolved behaviors that help them avoid such fates. They manipulate the leaves for protection as well as for food.

As you walk through the summer woods, watch for leaves that exhibit signs of insect alteration. You'll find that some leaves have been rolled. A caterpillar will have spun a mat of silk across the leaf's surface, and as the silk dried and shrank, it caused the leaf to curl slightly. More silk and more shrinking pulled the sides in further until eventually the leaf rolled up. Several types of moth and butterfly larvae are leaf-rollers—as are certain beetle larvae.

Other leaves will be folded. This is a variation on rolled leaves in which the leaf is merely folded over and secured with silk. Leaf-folders are mainly moth and butterfly larvae.

Some caterpillars tie several leaves together and are known as leaf-tiers. Look for tied leaves in sweetfern and in white pines where you will find pine needles tied into a tube by the pine-tube moth larva.

Leaf-miners are almost always the larvae of moths. They leave obvious excavation trails between the upper and lower surfaces of leaves. You can see, by the changes in the width of the trails, where the egg hatched and where the full-grown larva left the mine.

Leaf-miners are always tiny. But some leaf-rollers, leaf-tiers, and leaf-folders make worthwhile bait.

Summer

Midge Swarms

Most sportsmen have seen swarms of tiny insects dancing in a more or less stationary cloud either in the woods, out in a meadow, or near the shore of a pond or stream. The initial reaction to the sight is that they are a marauding band of mosquitoes out for blood and should best be avoided like the plague. That is a reasonable assumption, but it is dead wrong.

For one thin, the swarm is not necessarily composed of mosquitoes. It is likely to be a group of non-biting midges that look very much like mosquitoes but are entirely harmless. Secondly, even if they are mosquitoes, they are nearly all males, which don't bite. And thirdly, they are assembled for a purpose compared to which you are of very little interest—sex.

Many types of flies, including mosquitoes and midges, form swarms for the purpose of finding mates. The flies have spent their immaturity as larvae, often underwater. They pupated, and then emerged as adults. In the case of midges, the whole cycle took only about a month. Now, the adults must find mates, and the way they go about it is to form those clouds. The swarms are always located near some marker. The marker may be a tuft of grass, a patch of sunlight in the woods, a stump in the water, or your head while you are fishing. In any case, the flies' limited eyesight keeps them close to the marker and, thereby, in a tight group.

Both sexes join the swarm, but as soon as a female enters the group she is joined by a male, and they leave the group to mate. Afterwards, the female goes off to lay eggs, and the male returns to the swarm. At any particular time, a swarm will be almost entirely male.

The midges live as adults for only about a day or two, during which time they do not eat. New midges, however, are hatching out daily; so you may see swarms at a marker every day. Watching the behavior of swarms—the limits of their movements from the marker, their reactions to winds, the times at which they occur, types of markers, etc.—can be a productive pursuit during some otherwise unproductive time afield.

Milkweed

The milkweed is a plant that should be familiar to both the summer fisherman and the fall hunter. But neither has probably paid much attention to it. It's one of those swamp and old-field weeds that's so ubiquitous you haven't noticed it.

There are several species of milkweed throughout the country, but the most encountered are the swamp milkweed, which grows in wet areas, and the common milkweed, which grows in upland fields, old orchards, and along roadsides.

Look at the abundant, fragrant blossoms. They attract bees and butterflies like magnets, for the blossoms are filled with nectar. The plant needs the insects to transfer its pollen from one blossom to another. Yet if you look closely at a blossom, no matter how carefully, you won't see any pollen in it. Look instead at the legs of the bees on the blossoms. Sooner or later you'll notice tiny, golden saddlebags clipped to the bee's legs. Those contain the milkweed's pollen and will be left in other milkweed blossoms by the insects.

Look at the insects that live on the milkweed's leaves. Milkweed beetles are red and black; so are milkweed bugs. Tiger moth caterpillars are black, white, and orange. Monarch butterfly caterpillars are black, white and yellow. All of those insects wear colors to warn predators of the fact that they've been eating the toxic tissues of the milkweed and are thus toxic themselves.

Look at the seeds in the autumn pods. Notice how they're packed (see "Patterns"). Observe the structure of the seeds' parachutes.

Look closely at dead stalks of milkweeds in the winter. Notice how the fibers peel off in long, tough, silvery strips. Learn to recognize that material in the nests of birds, and you'll be surprised to find how widespread its use is.

Summer

Moths and Butterflies

All sportsmen are familiar with moths and butterflies, but the difference between a moth and a butterfly is often the source of some confusion. The explanation presented here may do nothing to remedy that, for in many cases scientists themselves disagree. We can make a few generalizations.

Both moths and butterflies belong to the same order of insects because both groups share the characteristic of having their wings covered with tiny scales. When you hold a moth or a butterfly by its wings, those scales will come off on your fingers and look like colored powder. The immature forms of both moths and butterflies are called caterpillars. Caterpillars of both groups specialize in eating and growing. Sight alone cannot tell you whether an unidentified caterpillar will become a moth or a butterfly.

All moths and butterflies go through a pupal, or resting, stage where there may be some differences between the two groups. Butterflies in the pupal stage form chrysalises, which are little, naked cases that usually are suspended from plants. There is no silk involved. Moths usually spend their pupal stage in a cocoon, which involves a good deal of silk. Some moths do not spin cocoons, but pupate underground.

Sometimes the adult stages are easier to distinguish. If you want to get technical, some moths have a frenulum, which is a bristle, or a bunch of bristles, on the forward edge of the hind wing that hooks onto the front wing and keeps the two wings synchronous when the moth is flying. No butterflies have frenulums, but not all moths have them either.

Butterflies usually hold their wings straight up over their backs when at rest. Moths hold their wings either straight out to the sides or tentlike over their backs.

The antennae of nearly all butterflies end in little knobs. Those of moths rarely end in knobs, but are either threadlike or feathery.

All butterflies are day-flyers. Most moths are night-flyers. You may find moths active during the day, but you will rarely if ever find a butterfly active at night.

None of the above is engraved in stone, but you should be able to hold your own against other sportsmen who haven't read this book.

Summer

Night Insects

Quite a phantasmagoria of insect life is attracted to lights at night, and any sportsman camped out in the woods is likely to attract an impressive assemblage to his lantern. Even in the relative security of a cabin or lodge, night-flying insects in striking quantity are bound to show up on the screens and around your lights.

Moths will probably make up the majority of insects attracted to your lights. Notice the variety. Some will be large and robust with hairy bodies and glowing eyes. Others will be small and delicate, looking like butterflies. They are almost certainly moths, however (see "Moths and Butterflies"). A few of the moths will have wings so narrow that they barely seem like wings at all. The fly tier should pay special attention to the various forms of moths.

A variety of beetles tends to be attracted to lights and usually makes their presence known by repeatedly bouncing against the screens. June beetles are famous for that. They are mahogany-colored, robust beetles about an inch long that are in the scarab family. As adults they eat the leaves of trees, but in the larval stage they are one of the types of white grubs that lives underground and eats roots. Another beetle commonly attracted to the lights is the stag beetle. It, too, is large and mahogany-colored but is easily distinguished from the June beetle by the impressive size of its jaws. It lives in decaying wood, and anyone who sees one does not have to be told to take care in handling it. You may also be lucky enough to attract click beetles (see "Click Beetles").

Depending on your proximity to water, a variety of aquatic insects will undoubtedly be attracted to your lights. Some of those will be large. Dobsonflies are likely to be on the list (see "What's What in Live Bait"). And some of the larger water bugs and diving beetles commonly home in on lights. Caddisflies also are attracted to lights and may show up in quantity. This, again, is a good opportunity for the fly tier to make some observations.

Those sportsmen who are particularly interested in insects will find a goldmine in light-attracted, night-flying insects. Those who are less enthusiastic about the subject had best leave their lights off.

Pitcher Plants & Sundews

Most sportsmen are familiar with the plant called the Venus' flytrap which is sold as a novelty plant that eats flies and other insects. Few realize, however, that the Venus' flytrap is only one of such plants in this country that eats insects. The Venus' flytrap is native to only North and South Carolina, and sportsmen are unlikely to find it in the wild because it is now nearly extinct due to collecting. But there are two other plants with similarly carnivorous habits that are abundant and widespread. The observant sportsman is very likely to find them.

The sundew is closely related to the Venus' flytrap. It consists of a single flower stalk bearing a small, white flower, and a rosette of reddish leaves covered with numerous stalked glands bearing drops of liquid. The rosette is usually no more than about two or three inches across; so this fairly small plant can be easy to overlook.

The glistening droplets attract small flies, but upon landing on a leaf, the fly finds itself stuck in the sticky material, which contains digestive enzymes. Over a period of several hours the leaf has a tendency to curl around the fly to put more glands in contact with the fly and speed the digestive process.

Another carnivorous plant is the pitcher plant. This is a much larger plant, reaching a height of a foot or more and consisting of several tubular leaves and a large, nodding flower. The tubular leaves fill with water, and they are rimmed at their lips with down-pointing hairs. When an insect crawls over the brink, it is on a one-way trip to its doom. Enzymes within the leaf mix with the water and dissolve the insect. The resulting nutrients are then absorbed by the leaf. Amazingly, there is a species of mosquito that breeds in the water within pitcher plant leaves and nowhere else.

Both the sundews and the pitcher plants live in wet, acidic, marshy or boggy areas that are deficient in nitrogen. The plants have poorly developed root systems, and their carnivorous habits provide them with the nutrients they cannot get from the soil. They still sustain the major part of their growth by photosynthesis, just like other green plants.

Both the sundews and pitcher plants tend to grow in colonies. If you find one, there will likely be others nearby. Additionally, since they share the same habitat, if you find one of these plants, look around carefully for the other.

Take a lesson from the fate of the Venus' flytrap and don't collect these plants. They are best observed in the wild, anyway. For a carnivorous aquatic plant, see "Bladderwort."

Summer

Solitary Wasps

When most sportsmen think of wasps, three kinds are likely to come to mind. There are the relatively gentle, brown, paper wasps that build the open, umbrella-shaped nests beneath our eaves. There are the yellow jackets that build their nests in the ground and are seen most often on fallen apples in the fall. And there are the highly aggressive white-faced hornets that build the large, football-shaped nests in trees and shrubs. All of those wasps have one thing in common—they are social. They live communally in hives, and each member of the hive has its own specific job.

Few sportsmen realize that the majority of wasps belong to species that are not social. They are, collectively, called solitary wasps because they do not form hives, and each female is responsible for her own egg-laying and providing for her offspring.

For the most part, providing for the young entails the paralysis of some living insect as a food source for the developing wasp larvae. Some species of solitary wasps, for example, seek out caterpillars. They paralyze the caterpillar with their stings, carry them to an underground chamber, lay an egg on the paralyzed caterpillar, and seal up the chamber. The newly hatched, larval wasp eats the caterpillar, pupates, and eventually emerges as an adult wasp.

Various species of solitary wasps specialize in different types of prey. Some hunt only caterpillars; others hunt flies. Some specialize in crickets; some in grasshoppers. Several types hunt spiders. There is an enormous wasp in the Southwest and Mexico that preys only on tarantulas. And there is a good-sized wasp throughout most of the U.S. that preys exclusively on cicadas.

All of the prey species are paralyzed and not killed so that they will remain alive and fresh while the young are feeding on them.

Solitary wasps range in size from very tiny to frighteningly large. Even the largest ones are surprisingly tolerant of humans and will allow close observation without alarm. Many make their nesting chambers in the ground, some excavate dead twig-ends, and a few build structures out of mud. Look for them.

Summer

Swallowtails

Every sportsman, no matter what region of the country he inhabits, has at least one species of swallowtail butterfly to observe. And that is a lucky coincidence.

Due to their large size (they are the largest of our butterflies), the swallowtails are undoubtedly the best-known butterflies in the country. There are about two dozen species in North America, and most of them share the characteristic of having tail-like projections on the hind wings that give them their name. But it is not just the adults that we should watch for. In fact the larval and pupal stages of these butterflies are of particular interest.

All caterpillars (the larval stage) of every species of swallowtail share a peculiar characteristic. While each species may look different, and while even different stages of the same caterpillar may differ greatly in appearance, each has the ability to extend from behind its head a yellow, fleshy, Y-shaped projection called an osmeterium. The organ is employed when the caterpillar is disturbed. This not only serves as a surprising visual display against enemies, but also gives off a peculiar odor. Close up and in full concentration, the odor is decidedly unpleasant. But in a much diluted dose, the scent is of apple or pineapple. Some beetles, interestingly, give off an almost identical odor when disturbed.

While feeding on their specific food plants, swallowtail caterpillars can often be found resting in rolled leaves of the host plant. The larvae of the spicebush swallowtail, found throughout the eastern two-thirds of the country, have false eyespots on their backs that disguise them as snakes. They are found primarily on sassafras.

Swallowtail pupae (chrysalises) do not dangle from plants like most other butterflies. They are secured to stems and fenceposts by a silk safety-belt around their middles, much like telephone linesmen.

Summer

Tiger Beetles

Both freshwater fishermen and surfcasters should be on the lookout for tiger beetles during the summer. You may even have seen them without realizing it.

Tiger beetles are found most often in dusty and sandy barren places like beaches and dirt roads. They are active only on sunny days. The hotter it is, the more active they are. As you walk along a beach or down a dirt road on your way to a lake, keep an eye on the ground about eight feet in front of you. You'll occasionally notice an insect that flies up and lands again about a dozen feet ahead, turning to face you. The impression you'll get is that it's a fly, for its flight is swift and delicate, not slow and cumbersome like the flight of most beetles. If you see one fly up as you walk, watch where it lands and try to stalk within observation distance. They are as wary as deer.

If you can get close enough, you'll notice the tiger beetle's long, slender legs. You'll also notice that the beetle is a brilliant, iridescent green or bronze, depending on its species. And if you can get closer yet, you may be able to see its formidable jaws. The tiger beetle is a predator of extraordinary speed and ferocity that will take not only other insects larger than itself, but even small crabs. The beetle catches its prey with its jaws, slams the victim against the ground until it's dead, and then sucks the juices from its body.

The larvae of tiger beetles, which you might be able to find in the same areas, are grublike predators that ambush their prey from holes in the ground. They are not nearly as readily seen as the adults.

Watch for the beetles now that you know what to look for. They're very common, yet relatively unknown.

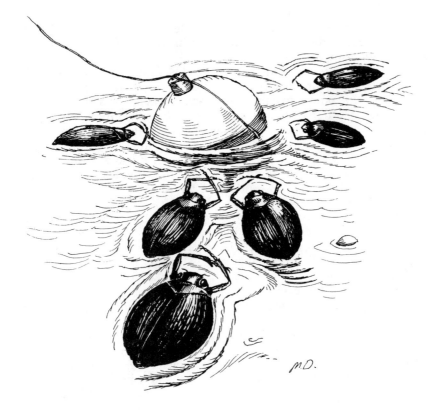

Whirligigs

Every fisherman has seen whirligig beetles (also known as lucky bugs) spinning in wildly erratic motion in small groups upon still waters. These insects are particularly interesting to watch while you are fishing from a boat or canoe in a quiet backwater.

Whirligigs rarely allow a close approach. One reason it's hard to get near them is that their vision is excellent. They are equipped to see both above and below the water simultaneously. Each of their two eyes is divided horizontally to give the beetle, for all practical purposes, four eyes. And because the beetle swims exactly in the surface film, one pair of eyes sees down into the water while the other pair sees up into the air.

In addition to its split eyes, the whirligig has a pair of short antennae. They are positioned on its head so that they ride exactly upon the water's surface, just as the styli in a seismograph machine ride on the roll of paper. Any slight ripple on the surface of the water is noticed by the antennae.

The whirligig eats other insects that have fallen on the water, and the antennae help the beetle locate prey by picking up the tiny ripples produced by a struggling meal. They also warn the beetles of the approach of danger. Watch what happens when you splash your rod-tip near the group.

It is also believed that the antennae pick up ripples that the whirligig produces itself. Those act much like the echo-location systems of bats but use water waves instead of sound waves. The beetle-produced ripples travel out, hit objects, bounce back to the beetle, and are picked up by the antennae. Thus, the whirligig knows by both vision and feel exactly what is nearby.

Notice how all those frantic whirligigs never bump into each other.

Fall

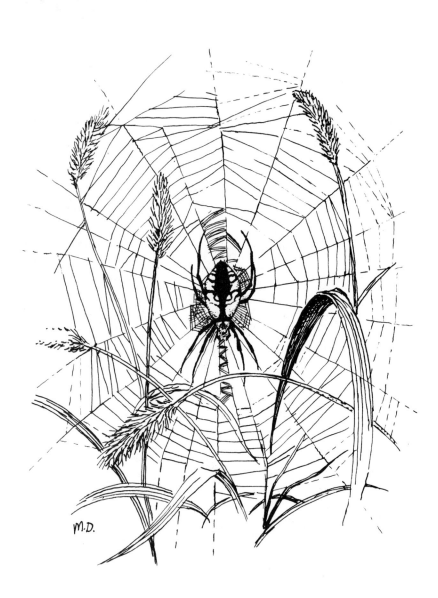

Argiope

The argiope, or golden garden spider, is the spider sportsmen are most likely to notice in late summer and fall. Not only is it conspicuous because of its size, coloring, and web, but it also likes to live in the type of areas sportsmen are most likely to frequent—grassy fields and meadows near water.

Argiope is one of our largest, web-spinning spiders. Females measure about an inch long, not counting the legs, which add about another inch and a half to the overall size. Their coloring is bright yellow with black streaks radiating from a Rorschach-like inkblot design. The male is only about a quarter of the size of the female and lives in a separate web.

The female argiope's web is magnificent, sometimes as large as two feet across. The familiar spiral, spider-web form, stretching across openings in the grasses and across paths, can be identified as the web of argiope even when the spider is not on it. Stretching from top to bottom is a pronounced zig-zag pattern unique to the web of argiope.

Argiope's great size allows her to actually pull grasses aside in order to make an opening for her web where she wants it. It also allows her to handle good-sized meadow grasshoppers.

In the fall, argiope lays her eggs in a case resembling a brown ping-pong ball, which hangs in the grasses all winter. The case is made of three distinct types of silk, and hundreds of overwintering babies can be found within.

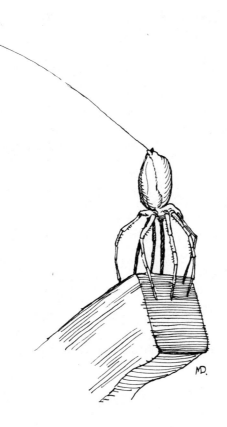

Ballooning Spiders

There are times in the fall when the upland bird hunter or the fisherman out on a lake will notice that the air seems filled with shimmering strands of silk. The light will catch the strands and reflect a display of rainbow colors as those on the surface of soap bubbles. We have a multitude of tiny spiders to thank for this dazzling effect.

Spider activity is at its peak in the fall, and the curious phenomenon of ballooning takes place. Myriad tiny spiders find it suddenly necessary to climb to the tops of grass stems, fenceposts, and other high vantage points. There they point their rear ends up into the air and release from their spinnerets a strand of silk that is drawn out further by the breeze. When the force of the breeze, the length of the silk, and the weight of the spider are all in the proper proportion, the spider is lifted from its launching pad and carried on the air currents for what may turn out to be miles. If the spider wants to descend for any reason, it simply gathers up its silken strand with its legs and, lacking any sail, falls to the ground.

Many of the silken strands that become obvious to sportsmen on bright autumn days may still be attached to their tiny passengers, or they may have broken loose. Curiously, there seems to be no certain explanation for the ballooning activity, though it appears to be quite widespread among spiders of many diverse species.

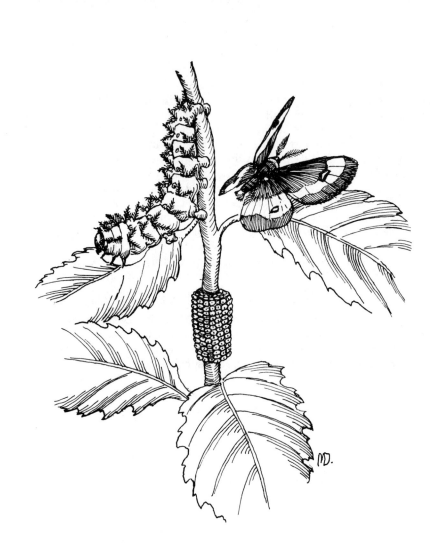

Buck Moths

While out in an oak forest or meadow during the warm days of autumn, the deer hunter, bird hunter, or late season fisherman in the eastern half of the country is likely to notice a number of day-flying moths, about two inches across, fluttering across the landscape. Because of their rapid wingbeat, the moths may appear as nothing more than a black and white blur with a touch of brick red mixed in, but the lack of grace in their flight should indicate that the insect is a moth rather than a butterfly—even though it is out in broad daylight.

The moths have been in their immature stages until now, having first hatched out of an egg that was part of a group of eggs arranged like a collar around a plant stem. Some may have been laid around a twig of oak, while others may have been laid around the base of a common, meadow shrub called meadowsweet. The tiny black caterpillars hatched last spring and immediately began feeding communally on the leaves of either the oak or the meadowsweet, depending upon which plant they found themselves. As the caterpillars grew, their abundant spines became obvious. Those spines, if handled, could produce a severe and painful reaction.

When fully grown, the caterpillars descended from the plant to the ground and, without spinning a cocoon, pupated underground. Now, in the fall, they emerge as adults, seek mates, and lay their eggs on the proper plants. The wings are black with a white, nearly transparent band from front to rear, and the body is black with a brick red tip.

There seems to be no reason for them to have been named buck moths other than the fact that they are most commonly seen during deer season.

Fall

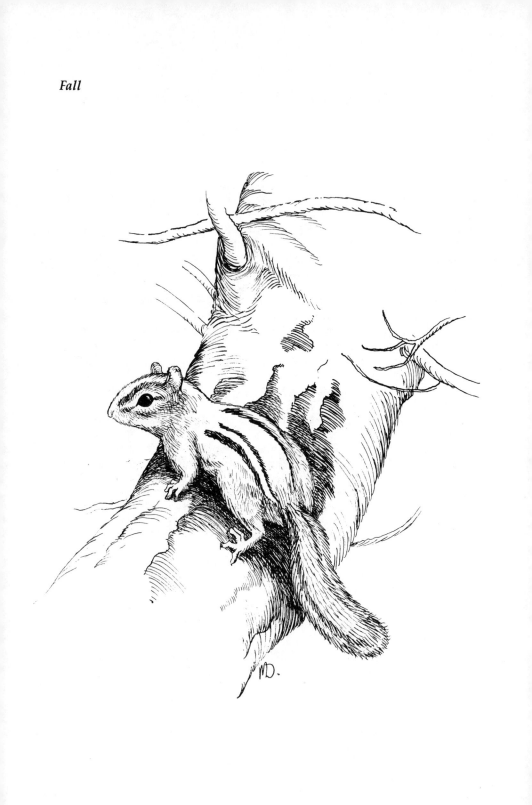

Chipmunks

Sportsmen out in the woods and fields in the fall are sure to hear a constant and persistent chirping sound that goes on, almost to the point of annoyance, for minutes at a time. The sound is like the peep of a monotonous bird that can't seem to stop or change its note. The sound is actually made by a chipmunk.

Chipmunks are familiar to everyone. They can be found, in one species or another, all over the United States and in virtually every habitat. In all of their variety, their habits and behavior are generally similar, though their coloring may exhibit great differences. Those that inhabit desert areas, for example, are extremely light in color, and their stripes are almost invisible. Those from the eastern and northern woodlands, however, are darker in color with sharply contrasting, dark stripes. In each case, their coloring provides the best possible camouflage.

Whether chipmunks hibernate during the winter is, again, a matter of locale. In the farthest northern and eastern portions of their range, chipmunks generally do become torpid for varying times during severe winter weather. But they are not usually regarded as true hibernators, for during periods of mild winter weather, even torpid individuals will become active. Chipmunks also are not known to store large quantities of body fat for the winter as do woodchucks. Rather, they store a winter food supply upon which they feed throughout the period.

Summer is generally a quiet period for chipmunks, and their activity is limited to early morning and late afternoon. That leaves the spring and fall months as the most active times for chipmunks when you will most likely encounter them. Spring is the time for mating and raising young, and the fall is the time for gathering and storing food for the winter.

The persistent chipping note so commonly heard in the fall is apparently a warning signal. Chipmunks are solitary animals and do not take kindly to the close approach of others of their kind during most of the year, and especially during the fall when food gathering is so important. In areas of relatively abundant food, the home range of an individual chipmunk is about a third of an acre. The chipping note seems to serve as a warning to other chipmunks that they had best not approach too closely or try to gather food from the area.

Fall

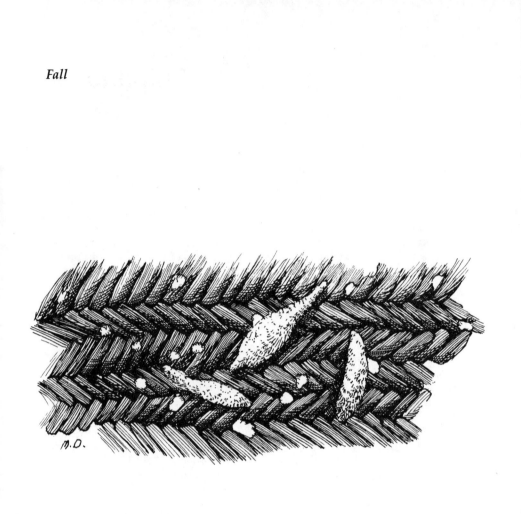

Clothes Moths

In anticipation of hunting, ice-fishing, and other cold weather activities, the sportsman is likely to unpack his woolen gear and encounter clothes moths. He will often not see the insects themselves, but merely the damage they have done. At times, though, the culprits may actually still be at work.

There are two types of clothes moths: the case-making clothes moth and the webbing clothes moth. The larvae of both moths do the damage. The adult moths, which are very small with only about ½ to ⅝ inch wingspread, do not eat. They merely mate and the females lay eggs. Those eggs are laid on our wool shirts, jackets, trousers, and blankets where the hatchling caterpillars can start eating in relative safety, comfort, and in the midst of an abundant food supply.

The eggs of the webbing clothes moth are laid by the adults in the spring and hatch in about six days. The larvae begin eating immediately and lay down a web of silk in the path of their destruction. After a couple of months, the larvae weave cocoons, pupate, emerge as adults, mate, and lay eggs. Then a second brood hatches and eats for a couple months more. This second brood overwinters in the pupal cocoon, and you may find them on the damaged gear in late fall.

The case-making clothes moth has only one brood a year. Again, eggs are laid in the spring by the adults, but the larva spends the entire summer eating and growing inside a tube that it carries with it. The caterpillar makes the case like a good pair of longjohns—silk inside and wool (from your garment) outside. It enlarges the case as it grows. You'll find them pupating in their cases in the fall.

Mothballs only keep the adults from laying eggs on your gear. Once the eggs are laid, mothballs have no effect on the caterpillars.

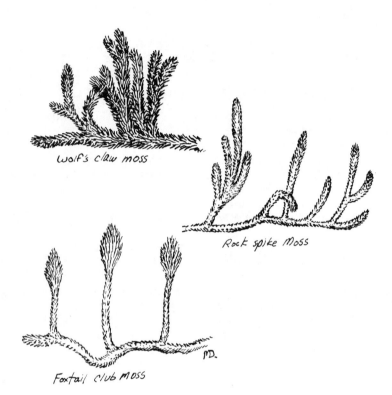

Wolf's claw moss

Rock spike Moss

Foxtail club moss

MD.

Club Mosses

Walking through the woods in fall and summer, the sportsman will notice low-growing, evergreen plants that look a lot like baby pines. In fact, club mosses are often thought to be young pine trees by those who are not aware of their true identity. But club mosses are actually non-flowering plants that are closely related to the ferns.

There are nearly two dozen species of club mosses in North America, and all share the characteristics of having small, evergreen leaves and a creeping habit. All are spore-bearing, and most grow cone-like strobiles that turn yellow in the fall when the spores ripen. Many species of club mosses throughout the country are used extensively in Christmas decorations.

The spores are particularly interesting and can be collected in quantity. The yellow spores borne by the strobiles are so tiny and numerous that they appear as a fine powder—so fine that a quantity in a small vial looks more like a liquid than like a solid. The extreme fineness of the spores makes a cloud of the dust extremely explosive, and the spores have long been used in various kinds of fireworks. Pharmacies have used the spores in the packaging of pills and capsules to keep them from sticking together.

Even more interesting is the effect obtained from sprinkling a pinch of the powdery spores on the surface of a glass of water. The fine powder so enhances the surface film of the water that it is all but impossible to get your finger wet through the film.

Fall

Daylight Periodicity

Spring peepers in October? The woodcock hunter in the autumn wetlands and the angler near the marshy shallows may begin to doubt their senses of hearing. Yet they may well be hearing peepers in the fall—and seeing other spring phenomena as well.

The return of warmth does not necessarily set things off in the spring. All sportsmen, particularly trout fishermen, know how fickle the spring weather patterns are. If leaf-buds, flowers, peepers, mayflies, and birds relied on the air and water temperatures for their spring schedules, whole populations would be wiped out annually by vicissitudes in the weather.

But even in spring there is a constant and stable clock on which all the above phenomena can rely; and that is day-length, the relative proportion of daylight to darkness. That is primarily what triggers the singing of the peepers, the return of the birds, the emergence of insects, and the blooming of flowers. When there is a certain amount of daylight (in terms of hours, not brightness) in the spring, things begin to happen.

By June 21st, the hours of daylight have increased to their maximum and begin to decrease once again. By mid-fall, daylengths are the same as they were in mid-spring and, in many cases, the effect is the same.

So hearing spring peepers in autumn should not be too surprising. Listen for the calls of other spring frogs as well. And watch for a resurgence of dandelions in lawns and meadows. Robins may start singing again before flying south. All is due to the periodicity of daylight.

Fall

Fall Colors

It is hunting season, and the woods are ablaze with color. This riot of reds, yellows, oranges, and purples is so much a part of the sportsman's autumn experience that hunting can hardly be imagined without it. Yet fall colors often remain, to the sportsman, merely a background stage-set. Try thinking of them more as individual players.

Trees don't turn random colors haphazardly. Each species of tree turns a special color every fall, and stands of hardwood species can be identified by their autumn colors from clear across a lake or valley.

During the spring and summer months, most leaves are green because they are filled with chlorophyll, a green substance that reacts with air, water, and light to produce food for the plant. In the fall, though, the trees cut off the water supply to the leaves, photosynthesis stops, the chlorophyll disappears, and the greenness in the leaves goes away. Now the leaves' true colors, which were masked by the chlorophyll, are revealed.

Bright yellow and orange leaves are rich in carotin. That substance is responsible for the colors of carrots, butter, and egg yolks. Aspens, elms, birches, and hickories are also rich in carotin.

Anthocyanin is a sugar in solution that colors the sap and leaves of other trees. It works much like litmus paper in that it tends toward red in sap that is acidic, and toward blue in sap that is alkaline. Swamp maples, tupelo, dogwood, and hawthornes have acidic sap. Their fall leaves are a brilliant red. Ashes, sweet gum, and some oaks seem to have sap that is more alkaline, for their leaves reveal a distinctly purple color in the fall.

On the next page is a list of some common trees arranged by autumn colors. Recognizing trees by their fall colors, adding your own observations to the list, and making more subtle distinctions within each color will help you recognize specific types of trees and, thereby, habitats from a distance.

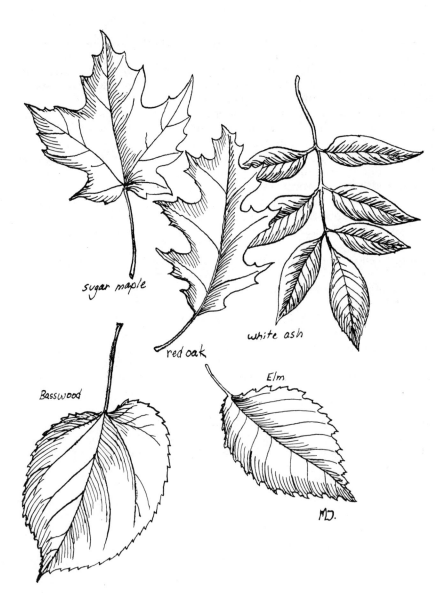

sugar maple

red oak

white ash

Basswood

Elm

MD.

Trees by Fall Colors

Yellow (Rusty)

pawpaw
hop-tree
buckeye
horse chestnut
witch hazel
elm
hickories
swamp white oak
black oak
scrub oak

Yellow (Bright)

tulip tree
ailanthus
striped maple
sugar maple
cherry
crab apple
shadbush
sassafras
mulberry
walnuts
hop hornbeam
beech
aspens
poplars

Red

mountain maple
sugar maple
red maple
sumac
hawthorn
dogwood
tupelo
sourwood
hornbeam
chinquapin oak
red oak
scarlet oak

Orange

mountain maple
sugar maple
persimmon

Yellow (Pale)

basswood
silver maple
box elder
locust
birches
willows
tamarack

Purplish

sweet gum
hercules club
ashes
white oak

Fall

Fall Webworms

Driving or walking along country roads and woody edges, the hunter will notice large masses of silken webbing in the ends of branches. He will be reminded of similar webs seen in the spring, and he may think that these, too, are the workings of the tent caterpillars. But the tents of the tent caterpillars are strictly a spring phenomenon (see "Tent Caterpillars"). In the fall come the fall webworms. They are different creatures.

You will have noticed in the spring that the tents of the tent caterpillars extend no further than the crotch of the branches. To feed on the leaves, the caterpillars must leave the tent. The fall webworm nests are in the ends of the branches. They enclose the leaves. These caterpillars can dine without ever leaving the protection of the web. As they consume the food supply, they simply expand the nest to include more leaves. Fall webworms, then, rarely if ever leave the nest until it is time to pupate.

Pupation takes place under bark or in leaf litter on the ground, and the pupa remains there all winter, emerging as an adult moth in early summer. After mating, the females lay their eggs on the leaves of apple, cherry, willow, and ash trees and cover groups of the eggs with white hairs from their bodies. After the eggs hatch, the young caterpillars begin building the communal web. By fall the nest is easily seen.

One would think that, because of their sheltered lifestyle, these caterpillars are well protected from all enemies. But if you give some time to observing the fall webworm nests, you may get to see how some species of hornets, with little regard for the protective webbing, make regular attacks on the colonies and capture caterpillars to feed to their own young.

Fall

Fungi

Fall is the season for mushrooms. The sportsman traveling through moist woodlands in any part of the country during this season will encounter hundreds of species of mushrooms and other fungi.

All mushrooms are fungi, but all fungi are not necessarily mushrooms. Fungi can be in the forms of molds, such as the green fuzz on old bread, the blue lines in cheese, or the white cottony growth on wounded fish. They can be in the forms that cause wilt in some plants, or in the forms of rusts and smuts on other types of plants. Or they can be in the forms of what we commonly call mushrooms or toadstools, either on the ground or on trees and stumps.

But even mushrooms are not quite what they appear to be. We have a tendency to think of mushrooms as the fungi themselves. But the mushrooms are actually just the fruiting bodies of the fungus, which is hardly ever seen. The real growing part of the fungus is called the mycelium. It lives in the leaf mold and in the rotting wood of dead trees. If you look under the covering of dead leaves on the floor of the woods, down in the leaf mold just below the surface, you will see a vast network of white threads. That is mycelium—the actual fungus. From that mycelium will arise spore-bearing, fruiting bodies that will be recognizable as a specific type of mushroom, depending on what species of fungus it is. So the mushrooms you see in the fall are really just a small, visible part of an all-pervasive network of underlying fungus that helps immeasurably in the breakdown and recycling of fallen leaves and dead wood.

The terms mushroom and toadstool have often caused a great deal of confusion. Both mean the same thing. Some people claim that mushrooms refer to non-poisonous fungi while toadstools refer to poisonous ones. The fact is, toadstool is just a cute name for mushroom, and both refer to poisonous as well as non-poisonous types. In addition, there are no easy ways to tell a poisonous mushroom from an edible one. You just have to learn to recognize edible and poisonous species the way you learn to recognize the difference between a rainbow trout and a brookie, or between a mulie and a white-tail. A mistake can kill you. Don't eat wild mushrooms unless you know what you're doing or are with someone who does.

Also note that there is a type of fungus that invades punky wood. By day it is entirely invisible, but at night it glows with a weird, greenish phosphorescence that is commonly called foxfire.

Goldenrod Insects

No matter what activity the sportsman pursues in the fall, he is sure to encounter goldenrod. The hardy, yellow flowers often fill meadows, overgrown fields, and old orchards. And along with being a nightmare to hayfever sufferers, they are a goldmine to a variety of insects.

A variety of beetles find the goldenrod blossoms an abundant source of food and come to eat the pollen. Because the blossoms of goldenrod are arranged in broad clusters, beetles find them easy to land on. As a result, both the flowers and the beetles benefit from the association, for while the beetles eat much of the plant's pollen, they also do a good job of cross-pollinating the plants in the process. Additionally, the beetles use the goldenrod plants as a kind of singles' bar where the finding of mates is a major activity.

One of the most common types of beetle to be found on goldenrod in the fall is the longhorned beetle. There are about 1,500 species of long-horned beetles in North America, and their larvae live in the wood of dead or living trees and other plants. The adults emerge in the fall and many species are attracted to goldenrods. Notice how many of those beetles are marked with yellows and blacks or yellows and browns. I suspect that there is some attempt to mimic the markings of bees and wasps, which are also abundant on goldenrods at this time of year. Predators may pass up the wasp-disguised beetles for fear of being stung.

One goldenrod insect that you should watch for is not even slightly concerned about bee and wasp stings. The ambush bug will grab just about anything it can catch, including honeybees, wasps, butterflies, and moths that are often many times larger than itself. It is most commonly found on goldenrods where its yellow and brown markings keep it well hidden.

The ambush bug is only about a half-inch long. Its front legs are in the form of grasping claws to seize other insects by the leg, wing, or antenna. Then it injects a fluid into the captive's body with its beak, which both kills the victim and breaks down its innards into a soup that can be sucked back out through the beak. You will often notice a curiously inactive honeybee on a goldenrod blossom that is being "eaten" by an ambush bug.

With the enormous abundance of goldenrod in the fall, watching goldenrod insects can easily become a serious alternative to mowing the lawn.

Fall

Grasshoppers and Crickets

Fall is the season for grasshopper and cricket activity, and all sportsmen who frequent grassy meadows will be aware of the presence of those insects either by sight or by sound. Both grasshoppers and crickets overwinter as eggs, so there are no adults in the spring. The insects hatch out of the eggs as tiny versions of the adults that are not particularly noticeable until they mature in the fall. In fall, however, the world seems filled with crickets and grasshoppers, and trout fishermen should be particularly aware of the extraordinary fishing possibilities. On streams that run through grassy areas, crickets and grasshoppers often miss their landing spots and plop down onto the water. Big trout take a particular interest in the insects' misfortune and hit the large stragglers with unusually splashy rises. Floating imitations or the real insects themselves make excellent bait.

All male grasshoppers and crickets produce sound as a means of attracting mates. Crickets produce musical tones while grasshoppers produce mechanical grinding or scraping noises. Regardless of the quality of the sound, each species has its own characteristic song and can be identified by it if you have an ear for such things.

The crickets and grasshoppers can be divided into two groups that differ somewhat in behavior and in the manner in which they produce their sounds. Short-horned grasshoppers have antennae that are shorter than the length of their bodies. They are the ones you often see flying up from dusty roads and rattling off with a dry, crackling sound. That sound is not their song but merely the sound their wings make when they fly. Their mechanical songs are produced when the insect rubs a row of tooth-like projections on its hind legs across a scraper on its wings. They are more active than other grasshoppers and crickets, and they mate during the day.

The other group includes the long-horned grasshoppers and the crickets, all of which have antennae as long as or longer than their bodies. This group is more oriented to specific territories, is more sedentary, and mates at night by making use of their long antennae. They sing by rubbing a set of ridges on one wing against a scraper on another wing. Females can be distinguished from males by the presence of a long ovipositor on their abdomens. Some species lay their eggs in the ground, and some lay eggs in plant stems (see "Tree Cricket Scars").

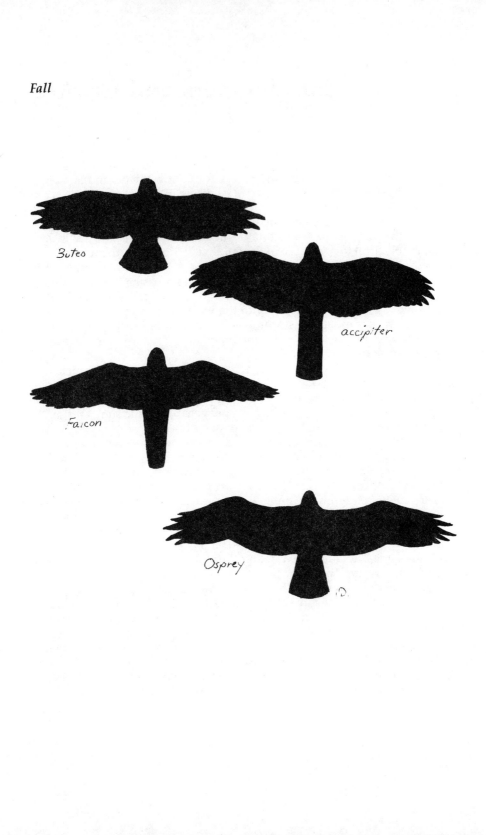

Buteo

accipiter

Falcon

Osprey

Hawks

Fall is the traditional time of year to talk about hawks because of conspicuousness during their fall migrations. Some areas of the country have gained widespread notoriety for the enormous numbers of hawks that pass through on their southward journeys. At such places as Hawk Mountain in Kempton, Pennsylvania; Cape May, New Jersey; and the north and south shores of the Great Lakes; literally thousands of hawks can be seen in a single day during the migration flights.

But the sportsman needs not visit those special sites to see hawks. Nor need he limit his hawk-watching to the autumn months. The hunter and the fisherman are usually in just the kinds of places that hawks inhabit, and they can be seen throughout the year in most places.

Although there are dozens of species of hawks with various ranges and habits, the sportsman can easily make sense of this group of predatory birds by learning just a few characteristics that distinguish four basic types of hawks.

First there are the buteos. Those are the hawks that soar to great heights. They can be recognized also by their broad, rounded wings and wide tails. Size is not a distinguishing characteristic. There are large buteos like the red-tailed hawk with a wingspan of four feet, and there are small buteos like the broad-winged hawk, which is the size of a crow.

The second, broad grouping includes the accipiters. These are woodland hawks that are distinguished by their short, rounded wings and long tails. Their flight consists of a series of quick wingbeats and a glide. The Goshawk, Cooper's, and sharp-shinned hawk are accipiters.

The third group is the falcons. These have the long tails of the accipiters, but their wings are long and pointed. They fly with quick, almost fluttering wingbeats. Among others, the sparrow hawk, prairie falcon, and peregrine are falcons.

The fourth group of hawks that sportsmen should learn to recognize is the osprey or fish hawk. It is a relatively large bird that is easily distinguished by the black, wrist patches on the wings. Its wings are also held in an arched or crooked position when it soars. Fishermen on large rivers and lakes may have the opportunity to watch an osprey at work. Any large hawk that is catching more fish than you are is probably an osprey.

Learning to identify species takes a good deal of time and practice. The average sportsman can get plenty of satisfaction out of simply being able to distinguish the broader groups.

m.D.

Jewelweed

Fishermen and woodcock hunters are likely to come upon jewelweed, for it grows in abundance in moist ground throughout much of the country. Often, a stand of jewelweed, also known as touch-me-not, will cover a large area of streambank. In the fall, when its seeds are ripe, the touch-me-not lives up to its name.

The pods of the jewelweed look vaguely like inch-long, green bananas. If you touch a ripe pod, the walls will curl back, much like a peeled banana ... but so fast and with such force that the seeds within will be thrown out in all directions. That's why they're called touch-me-nots. Any human or animal moving through a stand of jewelweed, will set the pods off by the dozens. So will the wind. Many will just go off spontaneously.

Try to let some go off in your closed hand so the seeds won't get away. You'll find them a delicious snack, tasting similar to butternuts.

Earlier in the summer, look closely at the jewelweed's dangling, orange or yellow flowers from which the exploding pods develop. All the male parts of the flower are fused together into a white, tooth-shaped part above the entrance. Bumblebees have to brush against it to get to the nectar back in the curled nectary. After the pollen is used up and carried to other jewelweed blossoms, the tooth falls off and uncovers the green, peg-like, female part that was inside. Now the female part can pick up pollen from the bees that are coming from other jewelweed blossoms. That's an unusual design for a flower.

The juice from the succulent stems of jewelweed has been found to be efficacious in preventing and/or mitigating the rash caused by poison ivy. Rubbing the juice on your body before heading out to the woods may prevent your getting the rash. If you've already got it, an application of jewelweed juice may be effective.

Fall

Migrating Monarchs

Monarchs are the large orange and black butterflies with which most sportsmen should be familiar. Their larvae are banded with black, white, and yellow, and are found eating the leaves of milkweed plants throughout the summer. By fall, those caterpillars have matured, pupated, and emerged from their chrysalises as winged adults. Now they begin their incredible journey.

It is difficult enough for us to understand how a bird the size of a warbler, for example, can leave its nesting area in North America in the fall, fly over all kinds of terrain including open ocean, and arrive at its intended destination, thousands of miles from its point of departure, on a different continent. But at least birds have bones. They are relatively sturdy little things with reasonably complex brains. We may find their migratory feats impressive, but next to those of the monarch, they are just ordinary.

The monarch leaves its place of birth as far north as Maine or Wisconsin or Ohio or somewhere in Canada and flies to the mountains of Mexico near Mexico City. Although this migration of monarchs has been recognized for years, only recently have scientists discovered that Mexican destination. There, millions of the butterflies cling to trees and each other and spend the winter. Then, next spring, they begin the return trip to their places of birth in North America, mating along the way, and laying eggs on the emerging milkweed plants.

By the time the adults from last fall arrive north again in the summer, they are in pretty bad shape. Their wings are tattered, their coloring is faded, and they will soon die. But they certainly cause us to reevaluate our thinking about butterflies as fragile creatures, for those monarchs fly a round trip of thousands of miles through all kinds of violent autumn and spring weather. The species not only survives but flourishes.

Watch for unusual numbers of monarchs in the fall. They are heading south.

Mockingbirds

The mockingbird is no longer restricted to the southern parts of the country. Like the cardinal, this bird has been steadily moving north and now resides in all but the most northern areas. Upland bird hunters have the best opportunities for seeing the unique, fall behaviors of mockingbirds, for it is in the densely overgrown thickets of orchards and hedgerows that the mockingbirds will be establishing and defending their fall and winter territories.

Birds do not generally establish territories in the fall and winter. Defended territories are usually associated with nesting and breeding, which most often takes place in the spring and summer. Breeding territories are established through behaviors involving visual displays and vocal signals that we call songs, and songs are nearly always produced only by male birds.

All of the above activities are shared by mockingbirds. But in addition to spring and summer breeding territories, mockingbirds also establish fall and winter territories around food supplies like berry bushes and multiflora rose thickets heavy with hips. Not only males hold these non-breeding territories. Female mockingbirds exhibit visual and vocal displays—including genuine songs—in establishing fall and winter territories.

Because few other birds are vocal in the fall, mockingbirds make themselves particularly conspicuous while establishing their non-breeding territories. The boundaries of individual territories can be rather easily determined through observation.

Watch particularly for two birds meeting on the ground, face to face, and performing a hopping dance. The dances occur right on the boundary line between neighboring territories. This serves to confirm the borders. The dances often end in a good fight.

Fall

Nuts and Berries

Acorns, hickory nuts, walnuts, beechnuts, chestnuts, pine nuts—all are the fruits of some of our common trees. All contain the future trees, and all have evolved the same dispersal strategy.

The deer hunter sitting silently in any stand of oak and hickory should know what that strategy is. He will most certainly be aware of the noisy activity all around him as squirrels and chipmunks frantically cache food for use during the winter. That's right. Trees that produce their seeds in the form of nuts have evolved that strategy to take advantage of the caching habits of nut-burying animals. Squirrels and chipmunks actually plant the trees' seeds. Because the average squirrel can remember where it has buried a nut for only about twenty minutes, large numbers of nuts remain planted. Those that are eaten are found by the animal's keen sense of smell, not by its memory.

Similarly, plants that have berries as their fruits have evolved that container for their seeds in order to take advantage of the seed dispersing capabilities of birds. The grouse hunter will have plenty of opportunity to observe that strategy at work, for he will be in prime habitat for many types of berry-bearing plants. A large part of the diet of the ruffed grouse consists of berries, and so do the diets of robins, starlings, cedar waxwings, bobwhite quails, turkeys, crows, and dozens of songbirds—nearly every one of which particularly relishes the berries of poison ivy, one of the most successful plants in the country.

Birds eat great quantities of berries that contain great quantities of indigestible seeds. The seeds pass right through the birds' digestive systems and are left in the birds' droppings, often miles from the mother plant. It's a great system that is evident from the large number of successful plants that employ it.

Seed Dispersal

Ruffed grouse live in just the right places for the sportsman to discover the breadth of the ingenuity of plants for getting their seeds dispersed. It is the weedy, overgrown fields and abandoned orchards that display the greatest variety of plant life and, therefore, of competition among species.

During the spring and summer, competition among plants is fierce for the agents of pollination. Each species displays the blossoms in the most effective way it can to attract insects that will effect the plant's cross-pollination. Now, in the fall, the products of that effort are mature, and the plants must ensure the dispersal of those seeds.

Look at your dog, your socks, your bootlaces, the hem of your jacket. You are sure to find examples of "hitchhiker" seeds. Plants like burdock, bidens, tick-trefoil, avens, and bedstraw equip their seeds with tiny hooks to catch onto the fur of animals and the clothing of humans.

Look in the air. Dandelions, milkweed, goldenrod, joe-pye-weed, thistles, and asters hang their seeds from parachutes so that the winds will carry them over great distances.

The seeds of ashes, maples, birches, pines, several other trees, and numerous smaller plants have wings to give the seeds just that added drift that will get them out from under the shade of the mother plant as they fall through the air.

Other plants have seed pods that explode, causing the seeds to scatter (see "Witch Hazel" and "Jewelweed").

Plants that grow near water, like cattails, willows, and American lotus make use of the water's currents to carry their floating seeds.

In most cases, an examination of a plant's fruits will tell you what method the plant uses for dispersing its seeds. What are the devices used by plants that produce nuts or berries? (see "Nuts and Berries").

Fall

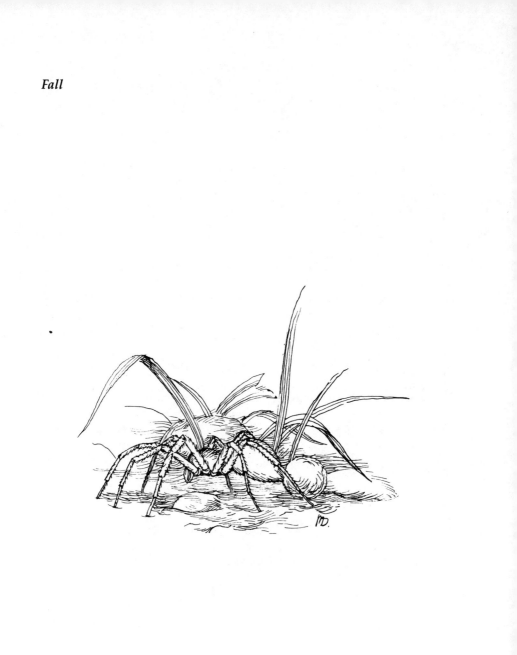

Spiders

Spiders abound in the fall, and sportsmen who are either hunting or fishing at this time of year are bound to notice their abundance. There are, of course, spiders around throughout the spring and summer, but in the fall those spiders that have hatched from eggs in the spring have matured, and they are engaged in the activities of mating and laying more eggs.

The webs of the orb-weavers will be the most conspicuous. Those are the webs that are designed on the classic spider web shape of a radiating system of spokes superimposed by a spiral. They are usually situated nearly vertically amongst grasses or in shrubs and are used to catch flying insects. Several types of spiders build that kind of web (see "Argiope").

On dewy mornings another type of web will make itself obvious. The webs of the funnel-weavers cover the short grass like patches of gauze. The funnel-weavers are fast-running spiders that weave a flat sheet upon the ground that has a funnel at one edge in which the spider hides. Flying insects are attracted to the natural landing pad the web provides, and the spider runs out to capture the arrival.

Many other kinds of spiders weave no web at all. There are dozens of common hunting spiders that rely on either their speed or their camouflage to capture insects by simply grabbing them. Crab spiders, which hide in flowers with their legs outstretched like crabs, can actually change color over a period of time to match the flower in which they hide. Jumping spiders, which look like miniature tarantulas, can jump several times the length of their own bodies to seize small insects that wander by. Wolf spiders, which are large, night-hunting, running spiders, have eyeshine like many other nocturnal animals when caught in a beam of light. The females carry their egg sacs under their bodies until the young hatch. Then the tiny spiderlings ride upon their mother's back until their first molt.

Some spiders manage to survive the winter by hibernating in protected places under bark, in wood piles, and under stones. They will be the spiders that make early appearances in the spring. But most of the spiders you see this fall will die with the coming of cold weather, and the eggs they lay now will hatch in the spring. The tiny spiderlings will take all summer to mature before becoming abundant again next fall.

Fall

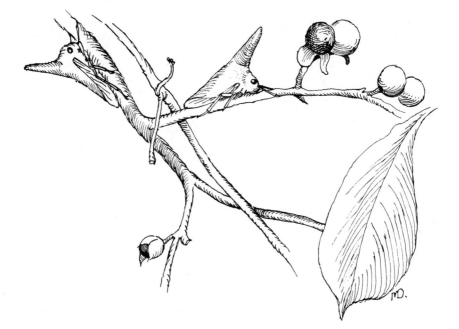

Thorn Treehoppers

Sportsmen of all persuasions will want to find these wondrous insects. Technically, they are actually called two-spotted treehoppers, but I have used a name that more graphically describes what you will be looking for. The thorn treehoppers are disguised as thorns, so well, in fact, that you may already have seen the insects without realizing it. Short of having someone point them out to you, the only way of discovering thorn treehoppers on your own is to be familiar enough with plants to realize that the thorned plant you are looking at is not supposed to have thorns.

Like all its close relatives (spittlebugs, aphids, cicadas, etc.), the thorn treehoppers get nourishment by sucking plants' juices, and the thorn treehoppers are fairly specific to certain plant hosts. Butternut, bittersweet, hoptree and locust are the plants preferred by the thorn treehoppers, but because butternut, hoptree, and locust are trees while bittersweet is a vine, it is usually easier to inspect the branches of bittersweet for the insects.

Bittersweet is a climbing vine that produces enormous quantities of red berries in the fall, with bright yellow casings that spread open but don't fall off. Branches bearing the colorful berries are often sold in decorative arrangements, but the natural plant is so plentiful in the fall woods that sportsmen will have little trouble locating it for themselves.

The thorn treehoppers lay their eggs under the bark of bittersweet vines in the fall by making a slit in the bark, depositing eggs, and then covering the silt with a white foam that protects the eggs over the winter. The little, eighth-inch patches stand out against the bark and are easy to spot. Where you find the eggs, look for the adults.

The adults really do look like thorns, for the area behind their heads is elongated in such a way that the disguise is remarkably effective and no doubt provides the insects with protection from predators and parasites. You will notice that, like real thorns, the insects are usually all facing the same direction on the stem. Turn one around and it will realign itself with the rest before long.

Fall

Winter Flocks

Curious things happen to some birds with the coming of winter. In summer, most birds will not tolerate others of their own species that are not either their mates or their offspring. Yet, with the close of the nesting season and the approach of winter, those same birds not only begin to tolerate others of their kind, but begin to actively collect in large flocks that may eventually number tens of thousands.

Crows are famous for that type of behavior, as are starlings. And there are certain places—a grove of trees in a particular park or cemetery, for example—that are used each night, winter after winter, as the roosting places of those enormous flocks of either starlings or crows.

Miles away from the roost area you can often watch small subflocks gather in the evening. Groups from six to fifty birds will fly in from all directions to a particular group of trees. Eventually that entire subflock will fly off to meet other large subflocks at the main roost.

It is believed that the nightly gatherings during the winter act as a valuable information-exchange. Subflocks that have found good feeding grounds communicate that information to other subflocks. Subflocks that have not had good luck at finding food can then follow a more fortunate subflock to the good feeding ground.

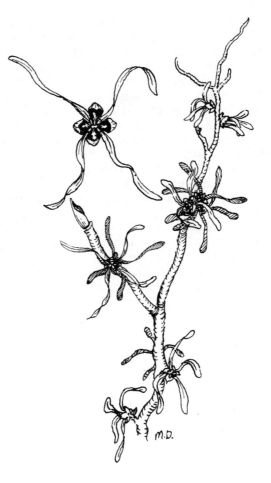

Witch Hazel

Deer season is also the season of the witch hazel, for it is in the fall that the witch hazel is putting on its show. The witch hazel, a woodland, understory shrub common throughout most of the country east of the Rockies, uses explosive pods as its method of dispersing its seeds. As each pod matures in the fall, it dries, shrinks, splits open, and suddenly shoots its two polished seeds out with enough force to send them thirty feet. A good-sized grove of witch hazel can produce quite a racket if the timing is right, and many a hunter has no doubt been fooled into thinking that there were small animals running through the dry leaves when, in fact, he was hearing witch hazel seeds.

At the same time the witch hazel is entertaining our ears, it is putting on a surprising show for our eyes as well. Witch hazel blooms in the fall, often after its leaves have already fallen, and its spidery yellow flowers, which will produce the seed pods of next fall, are usually the only blossoms to be seen in the otherwise wintry woods.

The well-known alcoholic lotion, used for soothing sore muscles, for cooling sunburn, and for numerous other healing chores, is made form a distillate of the bark of this plant.

Divining rods were traditionally made from the branches of the witch hazel as well.

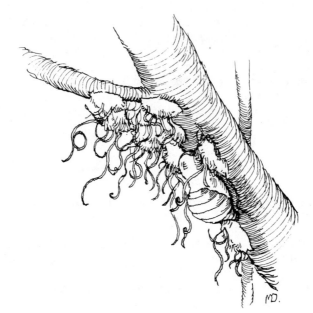

Woolly Aphids

The woodcock hunter is most likely to come upon the woolly aphids, for it is he who will be tramping the marshy lowlands amongst the alders. And it is only on alders that the woolly aphids can be found. They appear at this time of year as a batch of fluffy, white material on the dark and leafless alder branches, and they are worth a closer look.

First feel the white stuff. It looks cottony but feels waxy. It's produced by the insects you will find underneath it. The little, eighth-inch insects are covered with many tiny tubes through which they excrete filaments of the white wax. When several of these aphids group together, there is quite a mass of wax produced, enough to catch the eye of even the most absorbed woodcock hunter.

The aphids, by the way, beneath that protective woolly mass, are sucking the juice from the alder. At the same time you may find amongst them a very special caterpillar that is sucking the juice from the aphids.

There is a small brown and orange butterfly called the wanderer that lays its eggs in colonies of woolly aphids. The egg soon hatches, and the tiny caterpillar spins itself a protective case amongst the wool. Then it goes to work feeding on the aphids, incorporating their empty, woolly shells into its case for camouflage. Within two weeks it leaves the woolly mass and goes off to pupate. Its curious chrysalis, which looks remarkably like a tiny monkey's face, can often be found on the alder twigs near the woolly aphids.

The wanderer caterpillar is one of the very few butterfly larvae in the entire world that is carnivorous.

Fall

Woolly Bear Caterpillars

Whether you are bird hunting, deer hunting, squirrel and rabbit hunting, getting in some late-season fishing, or doing anything else that gets you out in the woods and fields during the fall, you will undoubtedly encounter the woolly bear caterpillar.

The woolly bear is a fairly large, heavily furred caterpillar that has a black band at each end separated by a reddish-brown band in the middle. During the early fall, most woolly bears seem to be in a great hurry, and the outdoorsman most often crosses paths with the woolly bear as the caterpillar is doing just that—crossing paths. The woolly bears seen during the hunting season are the second-brood larvae of the Isabella tiger moth. The first brood matured during the summer, and the adult female moths laid eggs. Those eggs hatched a few weeks ago, and the busy woolly bears seen now are from that second brood. Their apparent sense of urgency is real, for they spend most of their time during these last warm weeks looking for protected places to hibernate for the winter. Next spring they will continue eating leaves and growing. When they mature they will be the first brood of Isabella tiger moths of next year.

Try to pick up a woolly bear. Don't worry; the hairs are not poisonous as they are with some caterpillars. You'll notice that the woolly bear curls up into a ball. That posture combined with the nature of its hairs makes it extremely difficult to pick up and hold. It slides right out of your fingers and off your hand. That serves as a defense against predators.

By the way, although the old-wives-tale has been around for generations, the relative widths of the bands on the woolly bear have nothing to do with predicting the severity of the coming winter. I promise.

Winter

Bagworms

The hunter in the winter woods may notice some peculiar ornaments decorating the twigs of evergreens and the bare branches of shrubs. Some of those pendulous objects are over two inches long and invite a closer look.

What you will see is a little, football-shaped case hanging by a short, silken stalk and covered with twigs. The trout fisherman will be immediately reminded of the case of caddis worms, common upon the bottoms of streams and ponds. Of those cases in the trees, two types may be found. One has all its covering twigs arranged lengthwise; the other has its twigs arranged crosswise. Each represents a different species of bagworm.

The bagworm is the larva of a particular type of moth that you are unlikely ever to see in its adult stage. The adult female is a wingless, often legless, mouthless, and eyeless moth that never leaves her bag except to die. Hers is not one of the more glamorous lives on this planet. She is an organism stripped down for nothing but egg production. After pupating, the males emerge from their bags, find females, and mate with them in the females' bags. The females lay eggs right inside their bags and then crawl out and die.

When you find the bags hanging from branches in the winter, open them up and look inside. If the bag is empty, it was the bag of a male— for if the bag had belonged to a female, it will contain the eggs she laid inside.

Eggs unmolested by curious sportsmen will hatch in the spring. The tiny caterpillars will build tiny bags around themselves, carrying them around and enlarging them as they grow. By next fall the larvae will have become fullgrown, attached their bags to the trees, pupated, emerged, mated, laid eggs in the bags, and died—leaving the bags to be found by next winter's hunters.

Cattail Moths

Next time you are out duck hunting in the winter marshes, look at the cattails. Most of them will look like bursting mattresses as the seed-heads begin to fall apart and send the fluffy seeds away on the wind and water. That is the way they are supposed to look at this time of year. But you will also notice that a few of the cattails are not falling apart. Some look nearly as solid and compact as they did during the summer.

After you set out your decoys, break off one or two of those solid-looking cattail heads and take them back to your blind. While you are waiting for the ducks, you can make an interesting discovery.

Carefully begin picking the seed-head apart. After you get it started, the seeds will billow off the stem like wool off a sheep. But look carefully, for within that mass of seeds and fluff you will find a tiny caterpillar that is nearly the same color as the fluff. It is the larva of the cattail moth, and the seed-head is its winter home.

That seed-head did not begin to fall apart like the others because the caterpillar had bound it together with silk. In that way it maintains a cozy home for itself all winter . . . unless, of course, some duck hunter pulls it apart.

Winter

Evergreens

Every northern sportsman is aware of the evergreen trees in the winter woods. The pines, spruces, firs, cedars, and hemlocks provide cover and greenery at a time when all other plants have lost their leaves. But have you ever stopped to look at the ground on a winter's day when the snow is not covering everything? The woods are full of small, evergreen plants that are collectively referred to as groundcover.

One of the most common types of evergreen groundcover is the club-mosses. They have tiny, scale-like or needle-like leaves and look like miniature pine and cedar trees. Actually, they are related to the ferns and reproduce by spores rather than by seeds.

There are also several kinds of broadleaved evergreens, many of which retain edible though not necessarily tasty berries through the winter. One plant with a good-tasting berry is the wintergreen, also called checkerberry and teaberry. The red, pulpy berry has a wintergreen flavor, as does the tea that can be made from the leaves.

Another widespread evergreen is the partridgeberry. The vaguely heart-shaped leaves grow in pairs along the creeping stems and bear a light line down their middles. The plant's red berries are pulpy and tasteless, but the beauty of this evergreen makes it a favorite for Christmas decorations.

Other common evergreen groundcovers include the cranberry, bearberry, evergreen huckleberry, snowberry, dewberry, bunchberry, trailing arbutus, periwinkle, pipsissewa, and others. In addition, there are a few ferns, like the Christmas fern, that are evergreen. And many small shrubs like the laurels and azaleas remain green all winter.

A close examination of the leaves of most of the evergreen groundcovers will reveal that, like the needles of the larger evergreen trees, they have a waxy or leathery texture. They are far more substantial than the leaves of plants that are not evergreen in terms of their ability to protect themselves from freezing and desiccation. That's why evergreens can retain their leaves all winter while other trees must let their leaves go in the fall.

While other plants must first grow leaves in order to start producing food for blossoms and growth, the evergreens can get a head start in the early spring. By blooming early, the relatively inconspicuous flowers of these plants will get the attention of bees and other pollinators before the season of fierce competition begins.

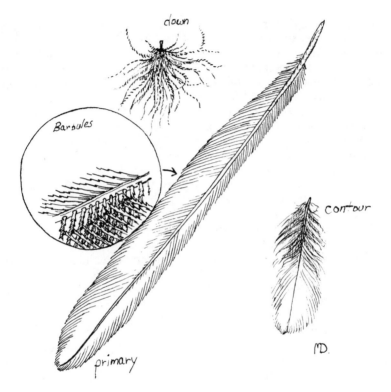

down

Barbules

contour

primary

M.D.

Feathers

The fly fisherman, the fly tier, the upland bird hunter, the water-fowler, and the bowhunter all come in contact with feathers. They certainly must appreciate the design of these marvelous creations of nature.

Take a look at some feathers through a good magnifying lens. The best feathers for that are flank, shoulder, or other contour feathers rather than flight, tail, or down feathers. Contour feathers are more likely to have all the different parts I'll be mentioning.

The stem or quill part of the feather is called the calamus. It is mostly hollow, and through it were delivered the nutrients and pigments for the feather as it was developing.

The calamus narrows down to become the center midrib of the feather and is called the shaft or rhachis. To the shaft is attached the broad, flat part of the feather, which is called the vane. Close examination reveals the vane to be made up of a large number of parallel structures called barbs.

The barbs are all set at an angle to the shaft and are further divided into tiny, hairlike branches called barbules. Beyond this point you need a microscope to see any further detail, but each barbule is further provided with little curled, hook-shaped projections called barbicels and hooklets.

Notice how the barbs in the vane stick together, but can be separated with a little force. Now draw the separated part through your fingers and notice how it has sealed itself back together. That is accomplished by the barbicels and hooklets, which hook into each other, from one barbule to its neighbor, and giving the feather its flexibility while making it air and water resistant.

One other part, often found on contour feathers but not on wing or tail feathers, is the aftershaft or hyporhachis. That is a somewhat smaller, companion feather attached to the same calamus as the main feather. Sometimes it is as large as the main feather so that the feathers are double, but most often it is much smaller, usually appearing simply as a batch of fluff at the bottom of the vane. Fly tiers refer to it as poor-man's-marabou.

Below the contour feathers of birds are the down feathers. An examination of those will reveal that there is no shaft. The barbules come straight off the calamus. In addition, the barbules lack the little barbicels and hooklets, so the feathers can remain fluffy and formless, providing insulation between the contour feathers and the bird's skin.

Winter

Flying Squirrels

Outdoorsmen who are out in oak and hickory woods in the winter have a good chance of seeing flying squirrel tracks in the snow, but it is unlikely they will see the animals themselves. Flying squirrels aren't rare—they are quite numerous and widespread throughout the country. But they are so nocturnal and so arboreal that they almost never show themselves until it is pitch dark. Even then they rarely come down from the trees.

The squirrels don't actually fly. They have broad flaps of extra skin that stretch between their front and hind legs, along their sides, which allow them to glide long distances, usually between trees. Occasionally, the squirrels glide to the ground and leave tracks in the snow. That first "landing" track is very distinctive and often shows the skin flaps clearly. But whether it shows the flaps or not, the track is peculiar in that it almost always starts suddenly out in the middle of nowhere, as if the animal just instantly appeared out of thin air, which in a sense it did. Other squirrel tracks start at a tree and go to another tree. Flying squirrel tracks start out in the open and go to a tree.

There are two species of flying squirrels in this country: the northern flying squirrel and the southern flying squirrel. Both are very similar in appearance, and their ranges overlap broadly in the northern sections of the country. Although the northern species is just a bit larger than the southern, flying squirrels, in general, are small creatures, slightly larger in size but lighter in weight than chipmunks.

Flying squirrels nest in natural cavities in trees and in abandoned woodpecker holes. They eat acorns and nuts, seeds, buds, and fungi, but also insects, slugs, eggs, small birds, and small mammals.

You can discover the presence of flying squirrels in an area through the investigation of owl castings. Because flying squirrels are the only nocturnal squirrels, their skulls will be the only squirrel skulls to show up in the pellets of owls. A good book about mammals will help you distinguish the skulls of flying squirrels from those of mice, rats, and other rodents.

Flying squirrels may also show up at bird feeders, but only at night. If you keep a red, photographic darkroom bulb lit near your feeder, you may be able to see these visitors without disturbing them.

Galls

The late-season deer hunter and the winter hunter after snowshoe hare and other small game will most likely notice galls, for they are most easily seen when the leaves are gone. And the ice-fisherman, though not necessarily in the right place for seeing galls, will find them of particular interest because many contain live bait in the dead of winter.

Galls abound all year, but winter is as good a time as any to talk about them. Galls are usually caused by insects; some galls are caused by fungi. They come in many forms, but are most often some sort of swelling or growth on a plant—either on the stem, leaf, or twig—that is not natural to the plant unless an insect causes the plant to grow it. Only gall-causing insects such as certain species of wasps, flies, moths, and aphids can do this. Furthermore, each of those particular kinds of insects usually specializes in a particular kind of plant.

One species of tiny wasp causes a characteristic gall on blueberry stems. Other species of the same family of wasps cause about 800 different types of galls on oak trees. A type of moth causes an elliptical gall on the stems of goldenrods, and a species of fly causes goldenrods to grow a spherical gall on its stems. Another type of fly, a tiny midge, causes a beautiful gall on the tips of willow branches that looks like a pine cone. That one is a dead give-away, of course, because willows don't grow cones. And there are virtually hundreds of other common galls.

The insects cause the plants to grow the galls for the feeding and protection of their young. Within each gall, at one time of the year or another according to the life-cycle of the insect that caused it, will be found the grublike larvae of the insect (except for galls caused by aphids, which don't have grub-like larvae). Sometimes there are several in one gall, sometimes only one. Sometimes the insect found within a gall is a parasite of the one that actually caused it.

Regardless, fishermen should know about galls. They can provide live bait year-round in a pinch.

Hibernacula

Any structure built by an insect for the purpose of using it as its winter home is called a hibernaculum. The plural of that is hibernacula. Sportsmen roaming the woods and fields in the winter have plenty of opportunities to notice such things.

Generally, any single leaf remaining on an otherwise bare tree or shrub should be investigated. Hibernacula of many insects are made from leaves. Look particularly at the stem of any persistent leaf, right where it attaches to the twig. If the leaf is, indeed, a hibernaculum rather than just a leaf that happens to still be attached, you will notice a small amount of silk tying the leaf to the twig. Viceroy butterfly larvae make hibernacula out of aspen and poplar leaves. First they secure the leaf to its twig with silk and eat away the tip of the leaf until only a section of midrib is left and finally roll the rest of the leaf around itself. The purpose of the tail-like midrib is not known.

The large promethea moth larva also wraps itself in a leaf after securing it to the bush with silk, and the cocoons within their pendant hibernacula become quite obvious to the sharp-eyed sportsman in winter.

Much closer examinations are required to spot the hibernacula of some of the tiny moths that inhabit apple trees, but the hunter passing through an old orchard may find this minor hunt worth his while. The pistol case-bearer and the cigar case-bearer are small larvae that carry protective cases around with them. In preparation for the winter, the larvae secure their cases to the twigs of the apple trees and hibernate within. The cases of the pistol case-bearers really do look like tiny pistols. The cases of both types of case-bearers can be seen to contain silk, bits of leaf fuzz, and the caterpillar's own excrement.

Ichneumons in the Bark

The lucky and observant hunter in the winter woods may one day come upon a very large, dead insect pinned to the trunk of a hardwood tree as though it were placed on a pin and preserved in the case of an insect collector. How that came about is a remarkable story.

There is a wasplike insect called the pigeon tremex that has an impressive, inch-long stinger. That stinger is actually used for the laying of eggs, which the tremex does in the wood of maples, elms, sycamore, oaks, beeches, apples, and pears. It inserts the ovipositor into the wood to a depth of half an inch, and lays a single egg. The egg hatches into a small, wood-boring larva that bores down about three inches and creates tunnels in the wood by its eating. Sometimes the tremex gets her ovipositor stuck in the wood and dies there, but that is not the insect we are looking for.

There is another wasp-like insect called the great ichneumon, which is an impressive, two-inch insect with an additional four inches of ovipositor. Its main mission in life is to provide its young with the larvae of the pigeon tremex to eat. The females of the great ichneumons, therefore, seek out the trees in which the tremex has laid her eggs. How it knows which ones those are is a mystery. But an even greater mystery is how it locates the actual burrows made by the tremex larvae within the wood. Somehow it does, and with its four-inch ovipositor, which is about the thickness of eight-pound mono, it bores a hole into the wood, right into the borrow of a tremex larva. An egg descends down through the drill, and when the larva hatches out, it wanders down the tunnel in the wood until it finds the tremex. It attaches itself to the tremex larva, feeds off it as a parasite until it kills it, and eventually emerges from the tree as an adult ichneumon.

Female great ichneumons can be found in winter, pinned by their own ovipositors to the hardwood trees. They have been there since the summer and died on the job.

Winter

Mouse Nests

Any type of hunter passing through nearly any type of habitat in any area of the country is likely to run across the winter nests of the white-footed mouse. As long as there is vegetation suitable for a bird to build a nest in, there are the makings for a white-footed mouse conversion job.

Actually I am talking about deer mice as well as white-footed mice. The two species are at times so similar that only an expert can tell them apart. Nonetheless, they represent distinct species and should be considered as such. For our humble purposes, though, when I say white-footed mice, I mean deer mice as well.

The animal is a pretty little mouse about six-and-a-half inches long, nearly half of which is tail. It is deer-colored above and white below, and has large bulging eyes that enable it to see extremely well at night, which is the only time it is active.

In winter, when such things are easiest to see in leafless shrubs, you may notice a bird's nest that seems unusually spherical, as though the original bowl-shaped nest has been covered with a dome. That is exactly what has happened, and the white-footed mouse is the one that did it. If the original nest is one that already had a lining of finer material within a coarser, outer shell, the mouse may have simply crawled between the layers and pushed the liner up to form the dome. Most often the mouse will build its own dome of bark, leaves, grasses, and lichens. There is a single opening that can be closed from inside.

During the day the mouse may be asleep within. A gentle investigation will be harmless to both you and the mouse.

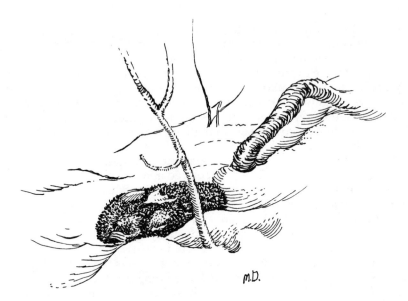

Owl Castings

On top of the snow, at the bases of large evergreens near the edges of open fields or frozen lakes, you can often find neat packages of fur and bones. They are called owl castings, and they contain the indigestible leftovers of an owl's recent meal.

Owls, especially large ones like the great horned owl or the barred owl, swallow their prey in large portions, bones and all. Powerful enzymes in the owls' digestive systems dissolve all of the digestible parts of a meal leaving only the bones and fur (or feathers if the prey was a bird). The bones and fur are later regurgitated in a compact mass.

The digestive enzymes are so strong and thorough in their work that they leave virtually nothing that can rot and stink. Picking the casting apart can be both enjoyable and educational. Often you will find the entire unbroken skulls of small prey animals such as mice, shrews, voles, rats, and flying squirrels. You will also find the jawbones and skull fragments of larger prey species like rabbits, skunks, muskrats, and cats.

Keeping an eye out for owl castings will give you an idea of the density of owl populations in an area. Examining the contents of the castings will tell you the types of prey species in that area.

Castings can be found year-round . . . but they are easiest to spot in the snow.

M.D.

Patterns

Any person who spends time outdoors can't help being struck by the seemingly endless variety in nature. The sportsman, particularly, is made constantly aware of the infinite variations in colors, shapes, patterns, and textures of the fish he catches, the birds and animals he hunts, and the plants and insects he encounters. Yet an even more careful look at those things will reveal a startling fact: that infinity of design is based on only a few, fundamental patterns.

The spiral is a good pattern to start with. How many natural objects can you find that are based on the spiral? Snail shells come to mind immediately. And so, perhaps, do the winding tendrils of grapes and other vines. But look at the scales of a pine or spruce cone. The rows of scales are arranged in spirals that run both clockwise and counterclockwise around the cone. Look at the center of a daisy or sunflower. The little florets are arranged in spirals. Notice the way buds grow on a twig; they spiral up around it. Fiddleheads, the new shoots of ferns, are obvious spirals. Eddies in water and dust devils in the air are all spirals. If you keep this pattern in mind, you will find dozens of other examples.

Another basic pattern to watch for is the explosion. This is a radiating pattern like spokes around a hub. Many wildflowers, like bedstraw and Indian cucumber, grow their leaves in radiating tiers up the stem. Queen Anne's lace grows its flower heads in the explosion pattern as do many other plants.

Watch also for branching patterns. Plants sometimes use an "opposite" branching pattern in which leaves, branches, or blossoms are paired opposite each other up the main stem. Other plants may use an "alternate" branching pattern in which the leaves, branches, or blossoms alternate from one side of the main stem to the other. River and stream systems exhibit branching patterns—also lightning bolts. The barbules on feathers and the tines on antlers are arranged according to branching patterns.

Another common, basic pattern is called the packing pattern. This one is best seen in a gob of foam. Next time you are wading a stream, notice that wherever three or more bubbles meet each other, a Y-shaped junction is formed. That pattern can be seen where things of similar size are packed together. Look at the kernels in an ear of corn, the scutes on a turtle's shell, or the scales of a fish or a snake.

Try looking at nature with those few basic patterns in mind. Naturally, not everything fits into those simple groups, but you will be amazed to see how many things actually do. Exercises like this tend to sharpen your awareness of detail.

Winter

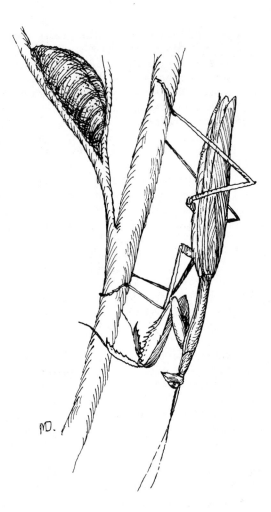

Praying Mantis Eggs

In the fields and old orchards where the hunter is likely to spend some time, the egg cases of praying mantises can be found. They are large globs of hardened, tan foam fastened to the stems of plants, fenceposts, and stones. They have been described as looking somewhat like roasted marshmallows.

The cases were made last fall by female praying mantises, some of the largest insects any sportsman is likely to encounter. The female mantis laid the eggs and excreted the foam all in one shot so that the eggs are not merely covered by the foam, they are surrounded by it. The eggs are thereby protected from freezing temperatures and wet weather.

In the spring, tiny mantises will emerge from the cases by the hundreds, and they will begin their ferocious predatory lives by eating any small insects they can catch, including each other.

Praying mantises get their name from the attitude of prayer they assume while holding their deadly hunting weapons at the ready. Their front legs are modified to form toothed, clasping grabbers that shoot out with lightning speed to grab and hold any prey that wanders nearby. Then the mantis eats its captive by chewing it up with its powerful jaws.

Luckily, praying mantises are entirely tolerant of humans, allowing themselves to be handled and examined. Female mantises are not always so tolerant of their mates, however, and have been known to devour them during the act of mating.

Shrews, Voles, and Mice

There are three kinds of small, mouselike mammals that are likely to be encountered by the winter sportsman. All of them are well-represented by a variety of species that can be found in nearly every section of North America, and all of them are similar enough in size and general appearance to cause even observant sportsmen a good deal of confusion.

Shrews are carnivorous and range from the two-inch pygmy shrew, which is probably the world's smallest mammal, to the four-inch short-tailed shrew, which is one of the very few venomous mammals in the world. Shrews are the most common mammals in North America. They all have pointy faces with tiny eyes, and in some species the ears are nearly hidden beneath the fur. They are active day and night, hunting insects, spiders, salamanders, frogs, reptiles, mice, other shrews, and nearly anything they can subdue. They spend much of their time just below the leaf litter and tunnel under the snow in winter.

Voles are often called meadow mice. They are blunt-headed, bullet-shaped mice that are also widespread throughout North America. They have small eyes, too, though larger than those of shrews, as well as almost unnoticeable ears. Their tails are always short and furred. Voles eat grasses and other plants and provide the most important link in the food chain between plants and meat-eaters. You can easily find their interconnecting runways cut through the grass in meadows and fields. They are active only during the day, mostly in their grassy tunnels.

Mice have large eyes, obvious ears, long tails and are active mostly at night. They eat almost anything. The white-footed mouse is discussed in greater detail elsewhere in this book.

The outdoor sportsman is most likely to see shrews and voles, for they are diurnal, extremely active, and more common than you think. In wooded areas, a hurried scurrying in the leaf litter may produce a quick glimpse of a shrew or two. In meadows, a brown flash through the corner of an eye will reveal a vole near the base of a clump of grass. The grass nests of voles can often be discovered by following the clipped runways. Indoors, in cabins and camps, sportsmen are more likely to encounter mice. They climb well, get into stored foods, and make their nests out of any soft materials they can find—including mattress and furniture stuffing, shredded newspapers, and insulation.

Shrews, voles, and mice all are prey to a multitude of predators including birds, mammals, reptiles, and even fish. But the particularly observant sportsman may notice an interesting phenomena—dead shrews in apparently perfect condition are often found on the snow. They have been killed by foxes.

Thaw Butterflies

Usually near the middle of every winter there is a period of warmth that we call the thaw. It is always followed by more winter, however, and has nothing to do with the approach of spring. Yet during those periods of thaw, the hunter can expect to find butterflies.

He can expect to find butterflies, in fact, on any sunny day in the winter, for warm microclimates often form on south-facing slopes and in rocky areas where the sun's warmth creates a small, localized thaw. Coming upon such an area, the hunter will find butterflies fluttering among the trees as if it were summer. These butterflies will always be of only two specific types—the tortoise shell butterflies and the angle wing butterflies.

For our purposes, the differences between these thaw butterflies are unimportant. The similarities are that their wings are sharp and angular in shape, are brightly colored on the top sides but camouflaged like dead leaves on the bottom sides, and they spend the winter as adults, hibernating in protected places.

The best known tortoise shell butterfly is the mourning cloak, a large brown butterfly with a noticeable margin of yellow along its wings. The best known angle wing is probably the comma, an orange and brown butterfly that is perfectly disguised as a dead leaf when it closes its wings above its back. A tiny silver spot on the underside of each hind wing displays the comma.

Because these butterflies hibernate as adults beneath loose bark, in stone walls, or in woodpiles, they can become active whenever conditions become favorable. Nearly all other types of butterflies spend the winter as either hibernating caterpillars or inactive pupae.

But despite this temporary warmth in the dead of winter, there are no blossoms to provide the butterflies with food. There is, however, tree sap. Trees respond to thaws as well, and abundant sap leaks from wounds in their bark. The butterflies seek out those fountains of sweet, often fermented, nourishment, and drunken butterflies are not an uncommon sight. When cold weather sets in again, the thaw butterflies simply go back to the protected places and resume hibernation.

The sportsman need not worry about having his stalk ruined by rowdy butterflies. No matter how plastered they get, they rarely get overly noisy.

Winter

Track Straddle

Normally, when learning to identify tracks, a person concentrates on the size, shape, and unique characteristics of footprints: a raccoon fore-paw looks like a baby's hand; a deer track looks like a heart; a red fox track has four toes and a V-shaped groove on the heel; and so forth. The raccoon print is about three inches long; the deer a little smaller, not counting the dewclaws; and the fox about two or two and-a-half inches.

Knowing those measurements and characteristics is fine and will pro-vide the hunter with important information when conditions are perfect. But how often does that happen? When the snow or mud is just the right depth and consistency for tracking, perfect prints are possible and every detail is apparent. But what about when the snow is a few inches deep and all you can make out is the trail left by an animal? At such times individual, clearly defined footprints are at a premium. The trick to making sense of such chaos is knowing the width of an animal's straddle.

As opposed to stride, which is the distance from the center of one footstep to the center of the one in front of it, straddle is the width of the trail from the left side to the right. An animal's stride will vary with its gate. If it is walking its stride will be shorter than if it is galloping at full tilt. But an animal's straddle is fairly constant, as it is governed by the width of its chest and, thereby, how far apart its legs are set. In situations where snow has been melting, individual footprints can become pretty badly distorted and exaggerated, sometimes increasing in size enough to turn a deer into a moose. But straddle size, even under those conditions, distorts comparatively little.

Here are a few, common, average straddle measurements to start you off:

Chipmunk: 2-3 inches, red squirrel: 3-4 inches, gray squirrel: 4-5 inches. Cottontail: 4-5 inches, snowshoe hare: 7-8 inches, jackrabbit: 4-5 inches. Skunk: 2 ½-3 ½ inches, otter: 8-10 inches, muskrat: 3-4 inches, raccoon: 3-5 inches, opossum: 4-5 inches, porcupine: 8-10 inches. Bobcat: 4-5 inches, lynx: 7 inches, mountain lion: 8 inches, Fox: 3-4 inches, coyote: 4-6 inches. Deer: 5-6 inches, moose: 10 inches. Bullfrog: 5 ½ inches, toad: 3 inches.

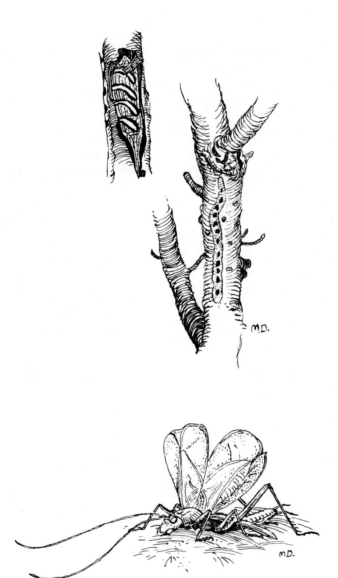

Tree Cricket Scars

If you are closely examining the bark of shrubs in search of evidence of deer or rabbit gnawings, you may also come upon a curious scar on those same branches. ·

The scar is about two inches long and looks like a partly opened mouth running lengthwise along the branch. Between the lips where the teeth should be is a zig-zag row of tiny holes that look as though they were made by a sewing machine. The scar was made by a pale green cricket about an inch long, and the tiny holes are where she laid her eggs.

By crawling along the stem and puncturing the new growth with her ovipositor, the tree cricket can lay her hotdog-shaped, yellow eggs well down in the pith of a twig. Each hole accounts for one egg. The mouth-like scar is the result of a chemical introduced into the twig by the cricket, which inhibits the bark from growing over the holes and imprisoning the hatchling crickets.

There are several species of tree crickets. One of them, the snowy tree cricket, has an extremely regular chirp. And since all insects are strongly affected by temperature, the cricket's chirp-rate varies with changes in the temperature. Count the number of chirps in fifteen seconds, add forty, and you have a close approximation of the temperature in degrees Fahrenheit.

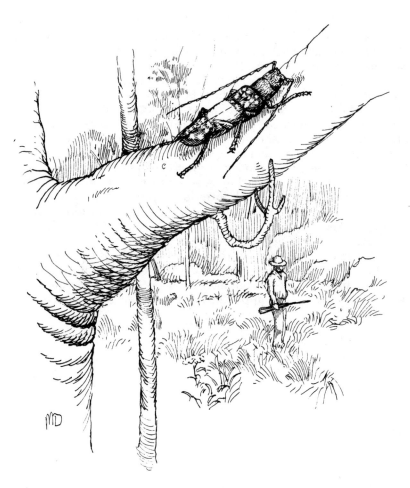

Twig Pruners

Only the most astutely observant hunter will have noticed the work of twig pruner or twig girdler beetles. The deer hunter on a stand in the late fall or winter woods, particularly in areas of abundant oak and hickory growth, is in prime habitat and in the perfect situation to appreciate these beetles.

But don't feel inadequate if you've never seen evidence of twig pruners or twig girdlers. Although their work is abundant, it is not apparent to the uninitiated, and you may have been looking at it for years without knowing what it was. Now you can change all that.

We are talking here of two different beetles that attain similar ends by slightly different means and on slightly different trees. But both types of beetles have the peculiar habit of laying eggs in twigs and then causing the twigs to fall off the tree while the immature beetle lives inside. The fallen twigs are easily distinguished from just any old broken twigs by examination. Beetle-cut twigs look cut.

Twigs cut by twig girdlers are cut by the adult female beetle. The female twig girdler, after laying her egg at the twig's tip, moves down the branch toward the tree and chews a groove around the twig until only a thin peg is holding it on. Sometime during the two or three years the larva develops within, the twig will fall to the ground and you can distinguish it by the smooth end with the little nipple remnant at the center.

Twigs cut by the twig pruners are cut by the larva. The adult female again lays her egg at the twig's tip, but that is the end of her job. The larva eats toward the tree, inside the twig, and when it reaches a point where the twig is about an inch thick, it begins to chew a spiral cut from the inside out until it reaches the bark. Then it retreats back up the twig and pupates for the winter. Winds soon knock the twig down.

So, in winter, girdler twigs will hold larvae, and pruner twigs will hold pupae.

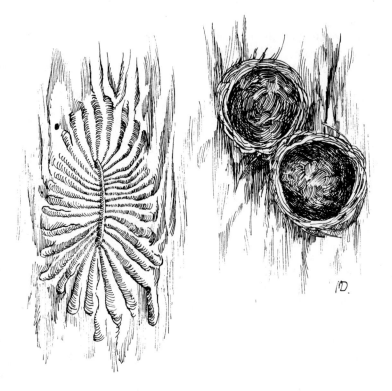

Under Bark

The ice-fisherman in particular will want to look under the bark of dead trees because there is live bait under there, even in winter. But all sportsmen will want to look under there as well.

You might find the carvings of bark beetles. Many form patterns that look vaguely like centipedes. There is a groove that corresponds to the body and many grooves perpendicular to it, but parallel to each other, that correspond to legs. Those grooves tell the life story of the bark beetles.

First, the adults bored through the bark, carved a little chamber in the wood, and mated. Then the female carved the single groove that looks like the centipede's body. Along the groove, at regular intervals, she cut little niches in each of which she laid an egg. You might see some engravings that look like zippers—just the long groove with the little niches—that represent this stage of the work. When the eggs hatch, the tiny larvae start to eat the wood, working straight out from the main groove. When they are finished, they pupate. And when they become adults, they emerge through the bark and fly to other trees. Their eating has created the legs of the pattern, and the legs got thicker as the larvae grew. Notice how they rarely run into each other.

Under bark you may also find the nests of the ribbed pine borer. Those are oval rings of shredded wood, about the size of a quarter, that look like tiny birds' nests. They are found under the bark of dead pines and are made by the fat, white, beetle larva that bores in the wood. When the larva is ready to pupate in the fall, it builds the ring and pupates within it. It soon becomes an adult beetle, but the adult remains within the ring all winter. Old nests take years to deteriorate if the bark has been undisturbed. So you may find empty nests, nests containing pupae, or nests containing adults.

For ice-fishermen, several other wood-boring beetle larvae overwinter under bark. Most are succulent and white and make terrific bait.

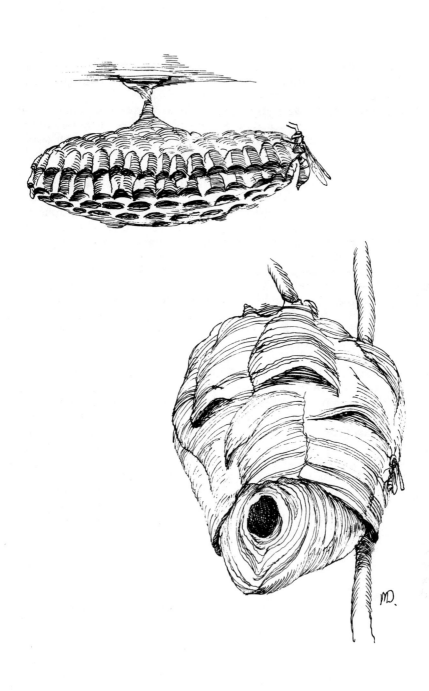

Wasp Nests

In winter, sportsmen can safely take a close look at the nests built by social wasps. At other times of the year, when the nests are active, some species of social wasps take strong exception to being approached too closely. In those parts of the country where large, dangerous animals are absent, some of the social wasps more than make up for that absence. Walking into a fully staffed hornets' nest in the underbrush can be comparable to running into a momma bear with cubs.

The nests are usually empty during the winter. They are, at least, empty of anything dangerous, though you may find an assortment of hibernating insects within.

There are two types of wasp nests that the sportsman is likely to come across. Both are built by social wasps that form communal hives in which there is one queen that lays all the eggs and several workers that take care of hunting for food, feeding the young, and enlarging and maintaining the nest.

One type of nest is a pendulous umbrella with a system of exposed cells underneath. The nests never get very large and are usually from one to six inches across. They are made by the brown paper wasps that are often seen around houses, often building the nests in windows and under eaves.

The second type of nest is an egg-shaped, basketball-sized structure that is often found hanging from the branches of trees or entwined in low shrubs. The wasps that make this kind are the white-faced hornets, and they are as aggressive as a pack of mad dogs. The structure of the nests, which you will see if you take one apart (in the winter, for heaven's sake), is more or less a stack of structures that are similar to the nests of the brown paper wasps. Each layer hangs from the one above it by little pillars, and the whole structure is enclosed by the egg-shaped covering that provides a single hole at the bottom for entering and exiting the nest.

In both cases, the nests are made entirely of paper. The wasps find suitable dry wood in the form of dead trees, fenceposts, barnboard, and the like, and they bite off small amounts with their strong jaws. The wood is chewed, mixed with saliva, and the result is paper slurry. Each wasp adds its share to the nest, and when it dries, it is paper. A close examination of a nest will reveal where different sources of wood were added, for slight changes in color will be plainly discernable.

Only the queens survive the winter, hibernating under bark and in other protected places.

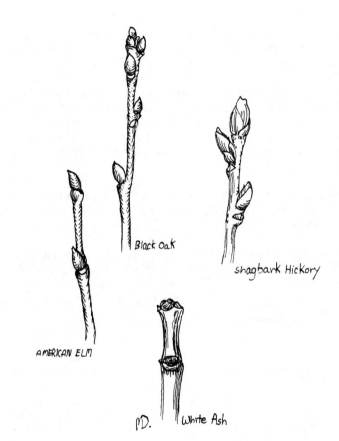

Black Oak

shagbark Hickory

AMERICAN ELM

M.D.   White Ash

Winter Trees

With the exception of evergreens, which have specially adapted leaves, all plants lose their leaves in winter where temperatures fall below freezing. We say they "lose" their leaves, but the fact is, they dump them in the fall.

Plants can sense the approach of winter by the decrease of daylength and by the lowering of the angle of the sun. That sets their clocks to triggering certain actions that will ultimately result in the falling of the leaves, preparation for winter, and even preparation for next spring.

Because winter is a time of drought (there is very little free water available in winter because most of it is frozen as either ice or snow), trees must turn off their water-lifting systems. The pumps for that system are the leaves. By evaporating water from the surfaces of thousands of leaves all spring and summer, the tree lifts a continuous column of water from the ground, through the trunk, out the branches, into the twigs, blossoms, fruits, buds, and out the leaves.

In turning off the water-lifting system, the tree causes a tiny band of cells at the base of each leaf-stem to loosen and dry out. To prevent an open, unprotected wound when each leaf falls off, the tree additionally causes the twigs to grow a corky, protective layer under the base of the leaf. As the corky layer toughens, it interferes with the leaves' plumbing. That cuts off the sap supply to the leaves and causes them to stop producing food. Their chlorophyll disappears, and the leaves change color. Soon after, they loosen completely and fall off. The tree is now ready to undergo a period of inactivity.

What happens in the spring? If the leaves are the pumps for the water system and also generate the food that provides the energy for flowering and growth, how does the system get started again without leaves? Well, the leaves are already there. They were grown last summer and stored away while energy was being produced by last summer's leaves. You can see them in the dead of winter, waiting for the lengthening days of spring to set them unfolding and growing.

Examine a twig from a living tree in winter. You will see the scars left by the fallen leaves. Close above each scar you will see a tiny bud. Overlapping scales usually protect the contents of the buds from the cold. Inside the buds are complete, miniature leaves. If you examine winter twigs from a variety of tree species, you'll notice that they all have their own characteristic scar shapes, bud shapes and colors, and other unique features that allows the observant sportsman to identify trees as easily in winter as in summer.

Contents by Subject

Birds

Insects

Mammals

Plants

Spiders

Miscellaneous

Contents by Habitat

This list is by no means engraved in stone. It is provided as a general guide so you can look up the appropriate subjects for the habitat in which you happen to find yourself while you are carrying this book.

Lakes and Streams

Wetlands

Fields

Woods

Woods and Fields

Select Outdoor Books

Hunting:

GOOSE HUNTING, Charles Cadieux
(208 pages, photographs, hardcover, $18.95 postpaid)
Stories of personal experience and facts about goose management and goose hunting are interwoven to make an entertaining and informative book. "The author has a way of making his point, instructing his reader, and entertaining him, all at the same time." Field & Stream

ALL ABOUT VARMINT HUNTING, Nick Sisley
(192 pages, photographs, appendices, paperback, $10.95 postpaid)
THE comprehensive book on varmint hunting. Everything varmint hunters want or need to know about chuck hunting, varmint rifles, improving accuracy on the range, and more! The woodchuck is covered in complete detail. Shotgunning for crows, starlings, and pigeons is also included.

Fishing:

BACKPACKING for TROUT, Bill Cairns
(208 pages, photographs, hardcover, $18.95 postpaid)
The founder of the famous Orvis Fly Casting School will help you get into remote streams, lakes, and ponds to catch trout. This very practical, informative book includes the latest in equipment and technique along with advice from regional experts.

ATLANTIC SURF FISHING, Lester Boyd
(160 pages, illustrations and photographs, paperback, $10.95 postpaid)
A completely illustrated guide to surf fishing up and down the Atlantic Coast. You'll find where and how to fish along with exciting and often humorous stories.

from Stone Wall Press

Conservation:

PLANT EXTINCTION: *A Global Crisis,* Koopowitz & Kaye
(256 pages, illustrated case studies, hardcover, $18.95 postpaid)
This is the most significant period of plant destruction in the history of
the planet. This book points out the causes, what is being lost, and offers
pragmatic solutions and what YOU can do. "This book should be required reading for everyone." CHOICE magazine.

VANISHING FISHES OF NORTH AMERICA, Ono, Wagner &
Williams
(272 pages, color plates and rare photographs, hardcover, $33.00 post-
paid)
The only current, illustrated, in-depth look at our endangered and
threatened fishes. Complete with rare photographs and color plates by
award-winning artist Aleta Pahl. The perfect gift for the serious
fisherman.

THESE ARE THE ENDANGERED, Charles Cadieux
(240 pages, photos and illustrations by Bob Hines, hardcover, $18.95
postpaid)
A dramatic look at the plight of our endangered wildlife, along with
current legislation and efforts to save them through agencies, parks,
zoos, and organizations. ". . . highly recommended for sportsmen, who
have a responsibility to protect wildlife." Sports Afield.

BACKWOODS ETHICS, Laura and Guy Waterman
Environmental Concerns for Hikers & Campers
(192 pages, illustrations, index, paperback, $9.95 postpaid)
Noted outdoor magazine columnists shed light on sensitive environmental issues with neighborly warmth and humor. "Outdoorsmen and
conservationists concerned bout the delicate balance between the use
and preservation of our wilderness areas should find this book of great
value." EnviroSouth.

If you can't find these books at your bookstore, outfitter, or gun shop,
please send your check or money order to

Stone Wall Press

1241 30th Street, N.W., Washington, D.C. 20007